PAM FARREL

7 SIMPLE SKILLS™

for

Every Woman

D0967470

HARVEST HOUSE PUBLISHERS
EUGENE, OREGON

Cover by Harvest House Publishers Inc., Eugene, Oregon

Pam Farrel is represented by the literary agency of Alive Literary Agency, Inc., 7680 Goddard Street, Ste #200, Colorado Springs, CO 80920. www.alivecommunications.com.

7 SIMPLE SKILLS™ FOR EVERY WOMAN
Copyright © 2015 Pam Farrel
Published by Harvest House Publishers
Eugene, Oregon 97402
www.harvesthousepublishers.com

Library of Congress Cataloging-in-Publication Data
    Farrel, Pam, 1959-
    7 simple skills for every woman / Pam Farrel.
    pages cm
    ISBN 978-0-7369-3781-8 (pbk.)
    ISBN 978-0-7369-4218-8 (eBook)
    1. Christian women—Religious life. 2. Simplicity—Religious aspects—Christianity. I. Title.
    II. Title: Seven simple skills for every woman.
    BV4529.F365 2015
    248.8'43—dc23

                               2014040392

Printed in the United States of America

    15 16 17 18 19 20 21 22 23 / VP-JH / 10 9 8 7 6 5 4 3 2 1

CONTENTS

To my precious Savior

From birth I have relied on you;
you brought me forth from my mother's womb.
I will ever praise you.
Psalm 71:6

To my beloved mom, Afton.

Thanks for giving me the rich foundation of simple skills
God has used to send some success my direction.
Your wisdom sown into the soil of my heart early
is reaping a harvest of blessings now.
I love you!

May your father and mother rejoice;
may she who gave you birth be joyful!
Proverbs 23:25

CHAPTER 1

Becoming Proactive

You picked up this book because you, like me, wish life were a little more simple! Or you, like me, want to get it and keep it together...but you may need some help finding out just what your *it* is! Those *together* moments seem few and far between. You know the ones. We catch a glimpse of ourselves in the mirror and think, *Wow! I really look and feel terrific!* Then we look around at our home, career, and relationships, and we feel on top of the world. Yes! We love those days when we feel we have got it and kept it together.

However, getting it and keeping it together might not feel all that simple. Maybe you have felt like my friend Lynne, who was having one of those days.

She had a to-do list a mile long and no way to get it all done in one day. While running from one errand to another, she decided to use her cell phone to call a girlfriend for some sympathy. The two friends commiserated over the desperate consequences of constant multitasking. As Lynne whined on the phone to her friend about her rough day, she arrived at her destination, gathered her purse, bags, and car keys, and shut the car door. Then she gasped to her friend, "Oh, no! Where's my cell phone?"

Her friend, caught up in the panic of losing something so vital, replied, "Did you look under the seat?"

Lynne reopened the car, searched, and said, "It's not there!"

The friend said, "How about checking your purse?"

Lynne dumped the contents out onto the seat, but still no cell phone. Exasperated and in a frenzy, Lynne shouted, "Lord, I've just got to find my cell. My son is going to call me any minute and tell me where to pick him up. Where is it?"

A pedestrian walking into the store overheard Lynn's frantic plea and said calmly, "You're talking on it, lady!"[1] *me*

Does Anyone Have It Together?

Getting and keeping it together can be a challenge—for all of us! If it makes you feel any better, some big corporations that pay people a lot of money to "get it together" still sometimes don't quite accomplish it, as represented by a few of these real employee memos:

"As of tomorrow, employees will only be able to access the building using individual security cards. Pictures will be taken next Wednesday and employees will receive their cards in two weeks." (This was from an international software company.)

A manager of an international shipping company is reported to have uttered, "What I need is an exact list of specific unknown problems we might encounter."

We are all in the process of becoming. Remember back to science class. Matter and energy are not stagnant. "The First Law of Thermodynamics states that matter and energy cannot be created or destroyed, but can be transferred from one form to another…The Second Law of Thermodynamics…states that usable energy in the universe available for work is decaying or running down."[2]

The same could be said of your life and mine.

If we are not moving forward,
we are sliding backward.

This book is the culmination of all the years of my life, ministry, experience, and the experiences of those who have mentored me and to whom I look up and emulate in their pursuit of success. Does this mean that I always have it together? Well, I try, but my humanity catches up to me too.

For example, let's just say math is not my thing. My father-in-law designed the engines that put men on the moon, my husband (though a pastor) was a math major, one son is a math teacher and coach, and our youngest is a mechanical engineer. But the gene in my DNA for math somehow mutated into "Let's have fun!" instead.

One day my husband was talking with our engineer son during his senior year in university. Knowing Caleb was required to build a race car to graduate, Bill asked him, "How's the Baja Bug Project going?"

Caleb said, "All right. I am on suspension."

Knowing our son was an honor student, I piped up, "You are on *suspension*? How did that happen? Who do I need to talk to at this university? You are a brilliant student; you can't possibly be on suspension!"

To which Caleb said, "Car suspension. Mom, I am building the car suspension!"

"Oh…" I mumbled out.

Yes, I am still working on keeping it together.

We are all in process.
We are becoming our best selves.

With a few simple skills we can become who God designed us to be and live the life God destined us to live.

Momma Said There Would Be Days Like This!

Awkward! is a popular term for describing the common emotion of feeling completely uncomfortable in our own skin. We all feel like that some days. Incomplete, unrefined, uncouth, or undone. The goal is just to feel less and less like the fool with the dunce cap in the corner and more and more like the the calm, confident, creative, woman God created you to be. To get there, we must be willing to appreciate the process.

All forward movement is good movement.

You can be your own best friend or your own worst
enemy. Choose wisely.

One of the first enemies of forward movement is ourselves. Our own stress can erode the lives we are seeking to build. Stress can make us feel like we are coming unglued. You might be stressed if you say things like this:

- I don't suffer from insanity—I enjoy every minute of it!
- I used to have a handle on life, but mine broke.
- I am not a complete idiot. Some parts are missing.
- I'm out of my mind…be back in five minutes!
- My wild oats have turned to Shredded Wheat.
- Failure is not an option. It comes bundled with my software.

Studies say that all of us feel stress. In a survey, 83 percent of Americans in the workforce reported feeling stressed.[3] A 2014 survey on *Women and Calling* from the Barna group discovered that 62 percent of moms were frustrated with the balance between work and motherhood; 72 percent of women said they had too much stress in life. Only 26 percent expressed that they were extremely satisfied with their quality of life.[4] And older people are less stressed than younger adults.[5] (Maybe the older folks and the 26 percent of satisfied women have learned some coping skills—and more importantly, maybe some skills to make the choices that can help one avoid some of the self-made stresses!)

Yes, just living in this imperfect world will be stressful enough. So the goal is this:

Don't create stress! Don't create drama!

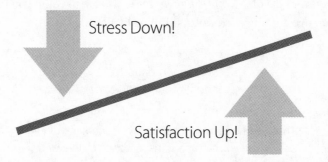

When we try living contrary to the way God ordained, life will be more stressful. It is the goal of this book to boil life down so even in the most complex situations, you will have the skills to handle whatever life dishes out. You must prepare and equip yourself for situations you can't anticipate.

But the journey to getting and keeping it together is a process. We are all becoming more skilled. And *7 Simple Skills for Every Woman* will make the journey happier, more enjoyable, and realistic to live out on a day-to-day basis.

Maybe you have seen or even have a poster with this famous quote on your wall:

Success is a journey, not a destination.

If heaven is our eventual destination, it should be our goal to be heavenly minded on Earth. It does matter to God *how* we live our lives, how we walk, and how we traverse down the road of our personal journey. God can give you an overcoming attitude:

> I have told you these things, so that in me you may have peace. In this world you will have trouble. But take heart! I have overcome the world (John 16:33).

> For everyone born of God overcomes the world. This is the victory that has overcome the world, even our faith (1 John 5:4).

It is the goal of *7 Simple Skills for Every Woman* to equip you to live out an overcoming, victorious, fulfilling life journey.

We cannot control life,
but we can control our attitude toward life.

I have learned on a sailboat that you cannot adjust the
wind, but you can adjust the sails to catch the wind.
—Dr. Gail Bones, *Living Crosswise*

Simply De-Stress

Maybe you are stressed right now. Take a moment to calm yourself. You will function better, make fewer mistakes, and be happier if you can live a little less stressed.

Try this. In a moment, close your eyes, breathe in and out slowly, and in your mind repeat this truth as if the Creator is whispering it to your heart and mind: "Be still, and know that I am God" (Psalm 46:10).

Anything under God's control is never out of control.
—Charles Swindoll

God has all of life handled. God has the ability to make your life workable. Not just workable but enjoyable! We will learn a little more about just why we can trust God with our lives in future chapters. But for now, just b...r...e...a...t...h...e as you take in this comforting truth:

> You make known to me the path of life;
>   you will fill me with joy in your presence,
>   with eternal pleasures at your right hand
>   (Psalm 16:11).

If God brings you to it, He will bring you through it.

Why All the Stress?

In America, the top sources for stress are…

1. Job pressure (coworker tension, bosses, work overload)
2. Money (loss of job, reduced retirement, medical expenses)
3. Health (health crisis, terminal or chronic illness)
4. Relationships (divorce, death of spouse, arguments with friends, loneliness)
5. Poor nutrition (inadequate nutrition, caffeine, processed foods, refined sugars)
6. Media (overload on television, Internet, e-mail, social networking)
7. Sleep deprivation (inability to release adrenaline and other stress hormones)

Half of you will handle these stressors by getting angry or irritable; almost as many will feel fatigued and lack energy. Many will get a headache, cry, or get a stomachache. But we can do things to improve the quality of our lives. How many items on the list above can we change by making positive choices? All of them! We might not be able to erase all stress, but to some degree we can reduce it. That is good news! Some simple skills *can* improve your life!

If you look at the world you will be distressed;
if you look within you will be depressed;
if you look at God you'll be at rest.

—Corrie ten Boom, Holocaust survivor

Decide Already!

Our life is the sum total of the decisions we make.

We will be talking about making decisions and choices quite a bit in this book. We must proactively decide where we are going, how we are going to get there, who is coming with us, what we will accomplish, and how we will adjust our attitudes all along the way. To be proactive, we must be skilled at seeing that a decision needs to be made and then making that decision. That will accomplish the healthy result we are looking for.

Maybe you have a friend or sister who struggles to be decisive—or maybe you're the one with the problem! Perhaps going to an ice cream shop with 31 flavors isn't delight but sheer terror because there are so many good choices. Does ordering at a restaurant become a 20-minute exercise in patience for your date or your family as they watch you weigh out every minute detail? And if small decisions are not difficult, perhaps it is the larger ones that put you into a stall pattern, making you "circle the airport" over and over again before you land on a decision.

Or maybe you are at the other end of the spectrum. Maybe you are impulsive in your decisions and you decide by your gut, your feelings, peer pressure, or some other impulsive motivation—and then often regret the choices you made. How can we land someplace closer to the center of these two extremes—closer to the center of God's will for our lives?

Whose Decision Is It?

Before you make a decision, make sure it is your decision to make. Is this situation one you are completely and solely responsible for? Will others be affected? Will they feel left out or will there be negative feelings toward you if their input is not considered? For each decision you make, do a quick check:

- This is my decision alone.
- This is a decision in which I want input from a spouse, parent, coworker, or mentor.
- This is a decision I would like to make after group input. (Who would you like in the group?)
- This is a decision I must make with another so we gain unity.
- This is a decision on which I will take the lead, but we'll take a vote as a democratic group.

Simply ask, "Who will be ultimately responsible for the outcome of the decision?" That person should make the decision. For the purpose of this book, we will assume that the majority of decisions we will discuss are ones you will bear responsibility for both making and answering for after the decision is made.

You can get in a lot of trouble if you make a decision that is not yours to make. For example, you might decide stopping at a red light isn't expedient for you. Too bad! Tickets and car crashes are ahead for you. At work, if you take over making decisions that belong to the owner of the company, you should not be surprised to hear, "You're fired!" In interpersonal relationships, say in a marriage, if you decide without consulting your mate that you will move to another state to take a job, expect a tsunami-sized emotional backlash!

Who Matters Most?

The chart below will help you prioritize whose opinions matter most to you in any given decision. Make a copy of this chart and try this exercise using a decision currently in front of you. It can be as important or inconsequential as you like.

List five people whose opinions matter most in this issue in box one. If you had to drop one person's voice, who would be the four remaining opinions? List them in box two. Drop another name and list the remaining three in box three. Keep dropping names and writing the remaining ones in subsequent boxes.

Box 1

-
-
-
-
-

Box 2

-
-
-
-

Box 3

-
-
-

Box 4

-
-

Box 5

-

What's the one remaining name in box five?

Did God appear on your list? His is the voice we all would be better off listening to, and this exercise is our way of helping you get to the heart of God.

Consider this: Your own wants and needs don't always take precedence. For example, if you are a parent, your children's best interests will likely take priority, or perhaps your mate's well-being or a parent's care will come before your own. That is why creating a "funnel" for the decision at hand, especially an important one, will be a helpful tool in discerning matters at hand.

Good Decisions Protect and Provide

In prioritizing people, good decisions will protect and provide for those who might not be able to, or yet know how to, protect themselves. To make it even simpler, let's use Jesus's own words:

> Truly I tell you, whatever you did for one of the least of these brothers and sisters of mine, you did for me (Matthew 25:40).

In the situation you're facing, who is the "least of these"? Who needs to be protected or provided for most? "The least of these" are the very smallest or least of status. Jesus said the way we treat those from whom we can gain nothing (and who may not be able to protect or provide for themselves) is a reflection of how we are treating Him.

If you are a parent, in every decision you make, your children are your "least of these." Ask, "How will this affect the kids?" or "What choice do I need to make to give the best long-range outcome for the kids?"

Does this mean the kids make the decision or get their own way? No! You make the decision by asking...

Who do I want my child to be as an adult? What choice
here will get them *there*?

And taking care of yourself might be in the best interest of your child. When you fly on a plane, the flight attendant gives instructions in case oxygen masks are needed. The most important lesson? "Secure your own mask first before helping others." If you don't take care of yourself, you won't be able to care for anyone else.

Who do I want to become? What choice here will get me there?

🌑 Always begin your decision-making by asking yourself how you can care for the "least of these." It will be easier to make a decision if you know whose benefit the decision is being made for. God will always encourage you to look around and see who needs the most protection or provision.

We will jump into other decision-making and relationship skills to simplify your world in future chapters, so for the remainder of this one, let's assume these decision-making skills apply for decisions you are solely responsible for making—at least for the time being!

Why Decide?

Are decisions necessary? Can't we just let life happen? You might have heard terms like *chillax, go with the flow, calm down,* and *lighten up.* There is a common misconception that if you make decisions, you are a driven, type-A personality. That does not have to be the case. Numerous benefits develop in a woman's life when she becomes decisive. First and foremost, decisions calm a life down.

I am sure you have tried to make a decision and suffered weeks of tossing and turning at night and mulling the choices over and over all day. Then when a decision is made, and it is the right one, everything calms down. This happens because...

Our emotions follow our decisions.

We must steer our emotions so they do not run their own path. The goal is to control our emotions and not have our emotions control us!

You control your emotions;
your emotions do not control you!

Because of our hormones, we women do have quite a smorgasbord of emotions. Some of those emotions are great, like love, joy, and excitement. However, some of those emotions can be a real thorn in our side. Like PMS.

PMS Does Not Own You!

Because our emotions are in a constant state of flux because of our hormones, if we are not diligent, our emotions dictate our lives. PMS, for example, can make us sound pretty outrageously out of control if we are not careful.

In the book *Why Men and Women Act the Way They Do*, I wrote an entire chapter on PMS, what makes it better and worse, and how to handle it so everyone in your world doesn't pay the price for your changing moods! And we girls do struggle with our attitude these few days a month, don't we? There are numerous jokes about PMS, including how you know you might have PMS:

1. Everyone around you has an attitude problem.

2. You're adding chocolate chips to your cheese omelet.

3. The dryer has shrunk every last pair of your jeans.

And do you know how many women with PMS it takes to screw in a light bulb?

One. ONE! And do you know why it only takes one? Because no one who lives in the house, not my dad, definitely not my brother, seem to know HOW to change a light bulb. They don't even know the bulb is BURNED OUT. They would sit in this house in the dark for THREE DAYS before they figured it out. And once they figured it out they wouldn't be able to find the light bulbs despite the fact that they've been in the SAME CUP-BOARD for the past SEVENTEEN YEARS! But if my brother, by some miracle, found the light bulbs, TWO DAYS LATER the chair he dragged over to stand on to change the stupid light bulb would STILL BE IN THE SAME SPOT. And underneath it would be the crumpled wrapper the stupid light bulb came in.

Hints for Surviving PMS

Let's make it simple. To survive PMS, try these three things that make an acrostic for PMS:

Pray for power
Make a plan
Seek some fun

Pray

You will feel on edge, bloated, irritable, anxious, and maybe even angry. Just because you feel like you have the flu and you've been hit by a bus doesn't mean you need to take it out on everyone else.

Ask God to help you choose to be nice even if you don't feel like it. Make a goal to be cheery even if your favorite jeans don't fit for two days. And don't use PMS as an excuse to get out of stuff (a workout, church, the dishes…). Even if you are not feeling 100 percent, do the right thing anyway. Besides, we can't let a little biology slow us down, right girls? Check this out—an American swimmer won three Olympic gold medals and broke a world record while at the height of her period. Pray and God will make a way for you to cope.

Make a Plan

Decide ahead of time to be proactive in handling your symptoms. Things that help are sleep, a bubble bath (or soak in a Jacuzzi), and avoiding sugary and salty foods (the exact things you are craving). And avoid soft drinks and caffeine. You are already amped up emotionally, so that venti mocha may just send you further over the edge!

Instead of fast food, eat salads, veggies, fresh fruit, whole grains, and lean protein and drink lots of water. And take your vitamins because calcium supplements and B complex vitamins will help you feel better. A study of more than 400 women showed that a calcium supplement each day cut PMS symptoms almost in half after three months. The B complex vitamins seem to improve mood and reduce bloating.

Another thing that might help is to record how you feel, logging information for four months. Every day, write down how you feel emotionally and physically. I just write a number on my calendar from one to ten, with one meaning I am in total near-death misery and ten meaning I feel fantastic! If you do this for several months you will know which days on your cycle are hardest. You can give yourself a little slack those days and give those you love a little warning that your harder days have hit.

You don't need to tell anyone the cause of your stress unless you want to, but if you do tell, keep it to your mom, your husband, your sister, or maybe your best friend. There is no need to tell a guy your cycle secrets until you are exclusively and seriously committed to him— you will know when because it will be in a situation where he will need that information, like a day on the lake, a road trip, or a trek home to meet his parents!

Seek Some Fun

Get active. In *Why Men and Women Act the Way They Do,* I quote some doctors' advice:

> Doctors don't know for sure why exercise helps PMS, but some believe that it helps stabilize blood sugar. Getting active may also increase endorphins, the body's relaxing hormones that are 500 times more potent than morphine. A brisk 20- or 30-minute walk three times a week seems to be enough to help most women. Exercise is one of the first things that the staff at PMS Access in Madison, Wisconsin,

recommend to the more than 2,000 women who call every day…Exercising helps women elevate their mood and ease anxiety.

Exercise reduces stress, raises serotonin levels, and increases oxygen in the blood and the blood flow, which helps reduce water retention. By strengthening muscles, it can prevent lower back pain and cramps. Doctors recommend walking, swimming, bicycling, tennis, or moderate jogging three times a week; increase activity the week before your symptoms usually begin. Studies show that women who engage in regular exercise—say 30 minutes of walking or aerobics at least three times a week—report milder symptoms.

Try to enjoy things you know you love on PMS days: time with friends, listening to praise music, or watching a funny movie.

If using the *pray, make a plan, seek some fun* method for living victorious over PMS doesn't work, consult a physician. God might want to team with the medical community for a more intense personalized plan to help you. The main point here is to be proactive and set your mind to live above any frustration or discomfort your period or PMS might bring. Join me in making the decision that…

Just because I feel bad doesn't mean I choose to act bad.

Make Menopause Madness Disappear

More than 4,800 women enter menopause in the United States every day. Perimenopause is the two- to fifteen-year span prior to menopause. For some women the perimenopause period may be short—only a year or two. For others it may be as long as seven to ten years, or even more. Some women in their late thirties and early forties may begin to show symptoms. The majority of women will begin to notice symptoms between 40 and 50. Twenty-five percent of women do not have any problems with menopause and manage the transition without assistance; 50 percent of women experience some menopausal symptoms, varying from mild to moderate. Twenty-five percent of women have more severe problems.

The average age for American women to enter menopause is 51. However, it can occur anytime between a woman's late thirties and her late fifties. The term "menopause" comes from two Greek words that mean "month" and "to end." Menopause is the absence of menstruation for 12 months. Menopause also occurs when a woman's uterus and ovaries are surgically removed.

When a woman is approaching the end of her monthly cycles, she begins to experience an imbalance in her hormones. Perimenopause is the time before menopause when levels of estrogen and progesterone decline. For some women, perimenopause can be worse than actual menopause itself.

Humor Helps!

Keep a good sense of humor as life transitions you forward. Here are some signs that you might be experiencing menopause.

- You sell your home heating system at a yard sale (hot flashes).
- Your husband complains about snow piling up on the bed (night sweats).
- Your husband jokes that instead of buying a woodstove, he is using you to heat the family room this winter. You are not amused (mood swing).
- You write your kids' names on Post-it Notes (memory loss).
- Your husband chirps, "Hi, honey, I'm home," and you reply, "Why don't you ever take out the trash?" (irritability).
- You find guacamole in your hair after a Mexican dinner (fatigue).

- You change your underwear after every sneeze (mild incontinence).

- You need the Jaws of Life to help you out of your car after returning home from an Italian restaurant (sudden weight gain).

- You ask Jiffy Lube to put you up on a hoist (dryness).

- You take a sudden interest in Wrestle Mania (female hormone deficiency).

- You're on so much estrogen that your husband of 35 years who has a receding hairline, an extending beltline, and is standing in his ripped undershirt with a wrench in his hand looks sexier than Brad Pitt, Mel Gibson, and Ricky Martin all rolled into one (hormone therapy).

Not funny, you say? Okay, the real symptoms are not as comical because they are real and can be a constant source of irritation. Your body (and your moods) may be changing so much that you barely recognize yourself.

Am I There Yet?

If you are still pondering if you are perimenopausal or in menopause, you can check with your doctor, or make a check mark next to the symptoms you might be displaying and take the list to your physician. Here is a list of possible symptoms of menopause.

- Hot flashes. Hormonal changes trick the body into thinking it is too hot. To cool itself, blood is rushed to the surface of the skin, resulting in a flushed appearance.

- Night sweats. Hot flashes that can interfere with sleep.

- Cold flashes. Sudden chills that make you feel clammy.

- Vaginal dryness, itching, and irritation. Lowered estrogen levels cause the lining of the vagina to become drier and thinner. This may result in painful intercourse.

- Urinary tract infections and the need to urinate frequently. Urinary incontinence can occur especially upon sneezing and laughing. (Kegel exercises may help.)

- Skin changes and increase in wrinkles. Decreasing estrogen levels make the skin less elastic.

- Mood changes and irritability. Mood swings, sudden tears, and even rage may be more likely in women who have had difficulty with PMS.

- Insomnia. Trouble sleeping is a common complaint of women in perimenopause or menopause itself. Night sweats may disrupt sleep. Irritability and depression can impair sleep.

- Irregular periods. Periods may become shorter or longer, lighter or heavier. Cramping may increase or decrease. Eventually, menses lighten, become less frequent, and then stop.

- Change in libido. A significant number of women report a decrease in sexual desire after the age of 50. This is matched, however, by an equal number of women who report improved sexual desire. Lower levels of estrogen and constant change in the way women's bodies function draws interest down. At the same time, more time with her husband, a greater level of privacy, the absence of any worry of getting pregnant, and the increased maturity in her own spirit can make sexual activity more appealing.

- Fatigue. This is the most frequently named symptom of women in menopause (and any other stage of life!).

- Feelings of dread and anxiety. Feeling ill at ease or experiencing feelings of doom is not uncommon.

- Difficulty concentrating, disorientation, and mental confusion. Some women experience difficulty with memory, attention span, concentration, or remembering specific words.

- Aching. Women often experience sore joints, muscles, and tendons, especially in the morning.

- Breast tenderness.

- Gastrointestinal distress. This can include indigestion, flatulence, gas pain, nausea, and sudden bouts of bloat.

- Exacerbation of existing conditions. Things you have already seem to get worse.

- Increase in allergies.

- Weight gain. On average, women may experience a gain of approximately 10 to 15 pounds in the years surrounding menopause, especially around the waist and thigh.

- Hair loss. Thinning hair on the head or the whole body is usually temporary in women and rarely of concern. An increase in facial hair is also usually slight and controllable by tweezing.

- Dizziness. Lightheadedness or episodes of loss of balance can occur.

- Changes in body odor.

- Depression. Yeah, because this list is so long!

The theme of my "Seasoned Sisters" ministry to women over 40 is *Choosin' Joy!* Because in spite of all these symptoms, the rest can be the best!

The key to making decisions in the menopause years is *stay steady*! Keep using the same wise decision-making tools you used in the early years, no matter how you feel! Remind yourself...

Faithfulness to God over my feelings!
My integrity over my irritations!

The Benefits of Good Decisions

We make our choices and our choices make us.
Healthy decisions create a healthy life.

This book is filled with healthy decisions and the simple skills to live them out. To be motivated to learn the decisions and the skills, most people are asking, "What is the payoff? Why should I do anything any differently from what I already do? Why learn to make strong, solid, and wise decisions? Why take the time to gain these Simple Skills?" Because...

Good decisions create the good life.

Decisions are good. Simply becoming a more decisive person will improve the quality of your life.

Why Decide?

Decisions give you more energy for the pursuits you care about. Solid decisions will make you more efficient. It is just more effective to choose well from the outset. Some people do not complete their "due diligence" before a decision, which can lead to the need to repeat. And continual unhealthy decisions will produce the need to do over, and over, and over, and over...again and again. Unhealthy choices are like being caught in a hurricane where the whirlwind will just pick you up, push you back, and flip your house over.

No time to do the right thing? Try finding the time to undo the wrong thing and then redo the right thing. Decide right the first time. Do-overs are very time consuming!

Do right so you don't have to do over.

Decisions simplify our lives. Our lives are an interconnected web of relationships. Decisions that are compatible with the way God designed life make relationships work better, create fewer negative consequences, and minimize the situations we need to clean up after the fact. As a result, good decisions develop a life where relationships need less maintenance. Good decisions help people trust us, so as an outcome, we can skip the complicated and time-wasting interactions that happen when we have to rebuild trust to rebuild a relationship.

Healthy decisions raise your confidence level. Anytime you are convinced that you are doing what you were designed to do, your focus, dedication, and motivation are high. There is simply no hesitation. You do what needs to be done. You say what needs to be said. When you are committed to healthy decisions, you research what you do not know and you get into action. There is no second-guessing, no what-ifs, and no over-analysis—you can soar!

Decisions Increase Quality of Life

Bill and I have a "business meeting" each year to delegate tasks that keep life running. Early in our marriage, I volunteered to clean and organize our home. I knew I wanted to be proactive and do this task as quickly as the professionals so I could get on to other, more meaningful activities. I learned four quick tips that have saved me hundreds of hours.

1. Make a portable cleaning carryall so all cleaning tools are in one convenient place and can travel with you from room to room.

2. Clean by task, not by zone, and clean each room top to bottom. Do all the same tasks before you move to the next one. Clean all the light fixtures and ceiling fans before you

vacuum! Pros say you can do an entire house in just a few hours.

3. Recruit help! Enlist your family to help and divide up tasks. Find or make a chore chart. Repeat after me: "I am the mom, not the maid!"

4. Never let the home get messier than your family can get straightened up in 15 minutes! This means training your family, "If you get it out, you put it away—right away."

If you are proactive in your home, you gain time because you are not hunting for objects. You also gain peace of mind because you are able to relax. Your plan for organizing and cleaning your home keeps it inviting for company, your family—and for *you*!

What Kind of Decision Maker Are You?

When it comes to decisions, there are three categories of women:

- Those who operate in HD (Healthy Decisions). These women mostly make decisions that are healthy and lead to productive, relationally satisfying outcomes.

- Those who operate in UD (Unhealthy Decisions). The decisions these women make are mostly unhealthy and shortsighted. They often find themselves in complicated situations and awkward relationships. Their lives are characterized by chaos and broken hearts and friends and family are left in the wake of their unmanaged lives.

- Those who operate in ND (Nondecisions). These women allow others to make decisions for them or they avoid making choices. Life runs them instead of them running life. This approach leads to codependent relationships, underachieving, emotional turmoil, missed opportunities, and immature interactions. The greatest risk of being

a non-decider is becoming vulnerable to toxic relationships, domestic abuse, or a life lived completely controlled
by someone overbearing, abusive, or manipulative—using
you for their gain or to fulfill some dysfunctional need in
his or her life by telling you what to do or not do.

No Excuses—Decide!

Women fall into several traps that slow the process of personal
growth and keep them from healthy decisions:

- They let others make decisions for them that they should
  be making for themselves.

- They blame poor decisions on others.

- They decide they don't need to make changes because
  "that's the way they've always been."

- They make excuses for not making decisions.

- They refuse to set priorities that could guide their decisions.

- They are too lazy to make the effort it takes.

- They give in to peer pressure rather than deciding what is
  best.

- They are not honest about the changes they know deep
  down need to be made.

- They go passive, with thoughts like, "After all, isn't it my
  husband's job to lead and my job to submit?" This skewed
  view of submission places a woman somewhere between
  a doormat and a puppy dog. (More on what is healthy in
  relationships will come later in the book.)

Which of these unhealthy decision-making patterns do you catch yourself falling into most often?

Rate your decision-making skill as it stands right now. Place a star on this continuum. One means you are indecisive and the majority of your decisions are made by someone else, or you consistently just don't decide and life and circumstances carry you. Ten would mean you are a decision-making rock star. You have clear focus, clear calling, and clear decision-making patterns that lead to strong, happy and healthy outcomes.

1 ———————————————————————————— 10

The Happy Life Decision Cycle

There is a wonderful cycle of decision-making that will prove to bring you deep lasting joy. Jesus tells us about it in John 14:21: "Whoever has my commands and keeps them is the one who loves me. The one who loves me will be loved by my Father, and I too will love them and show myself to them."

So the cycle is:

- We read a command of God.
- We decide to obey it because we love God.
- God shows himself to us. He manifests, reveals, and discloses His character, His power, His majesty—who He is!
- We are wowed by God!

Our response to this glimpse of God will likely be, "Wow! What an awesome God!" and it changes our heart and motivation. As God continues to show Himself, we become even more motivated to obey. Each time we obey, God reveals more of His wonderful love and character. A wonderful symbiotic relationship develops.

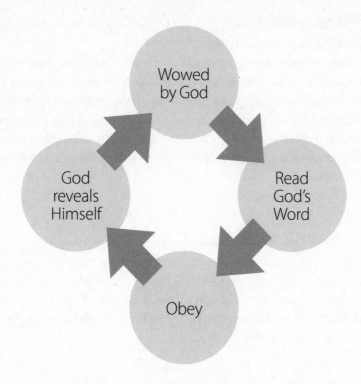

God shows His love to us and we show our love to Him and this makes our relationship with Him deeper, richer, and fuller! You and God become an unstoppable team: God with His power, love, and awesome character, and you with your heart, love, and obedience!

The first Christian book I ever bought with my own money was a poetry book, *I Love the Word Impossible,* by Ann Kiemel. One line, spoken by Ann's mother, set a solid foundation for my Christian life: "It pays to follow Jesus."

God shows His love to us and we show our love to Him,
and life keeps getting better!

The Retaining Wall

We live on a steep hill. During a torrential rainstorm, a piece of our property slid down the hill and into the street. Our land washed away downstream. This all happened because the previous owner had laid a retaining wall of brick that looked strong, but as we discovered in the rain, there was no foundation. While I have been writing this book, I have been watching my husband, Bill, pour deep footings into the solid rock secured with iron rebar. Brick by brick, he is building a solid new retaining wall. He has spent a few hours every day, little by little, laying each brick in its appropriate place. Like the Great Wall of China protected the inhabitants behind it, so our mini wall is protecting our land from erosion. It raises the value of our land.

Good decisions are like that. Brick by brick, one solid decision after another will keep our lives from eroding. Becoming a woman who makes solid decisions will build a secure, solid, and successful life.

Solid footings build a solid life.

This or That?

The journey of our life is filled with decisions. Every day we must make decisions about what food we will eat, how we will spend our time, and who we will spend that time with. Most of these decisions are minor in nature, but they come in rapid fashion. One result of the information age is a never-ending stream of data that requires almost constant decision-making.

Studies reveal that the average person makes approximately 5,000 to 25,000 decisions each day.

Decision-making can either take time or make time.

With the avalanche of decisions needed, you must be both efficient and effective to be able to enjoy the opportunities in front of you. In the book *The Compound Effect* we read, "decisions shape your destiny. The future is what you make of it. Little, everyday decisions will either take you to the life you desire or to disaster by default. In fact, it is the littlest decisions that shape our life. Stray off course by just two millimeters, and your trajectory changes...The good news is change is within you...a mere two millimeter adjustment can also bring you right back home. The trick is finding the plan, the guide, the map that shows you where that home is."[6]

Sometimes it is those first life lessons that come back to remind us how to proceed forward as adults. As a toddler, you quickly learned that if you piled one block onto another in a tall tower, that tower wobbled and fell. However, if you took the time and built the tower in a pyramid form with a solid base of blocks first, that structure was solid. The simple skills you learn in this book will be a strong base upon which you can build your successful life.

The first steps are often the hardest. So make a clear first step: Decide to get started in learning and using simple skills for success.

Take the first step in faith.
You don't have to see the whole staircase,
just take the first step.

—Martin Luther King, Jr.

Jumpstart Your Adventure

Many women talk about wanting their lives to change, but they never do anything about it. God gave us a few tangible reminders that action is vital to success. God told Abram to *go* to a new country. He told Jacob to *go* back to his family, *go* make an altar, and *go* to Egypt. He told Moses to *go* assemble the elders and make ready for a deliverance, *go* tell Pharaoh to free God's people, and *go* lead the people. And there are so many more! Yes, the Bible is full of commands by God to get up and go! Jesus pronounced one of the greatest directives to the disciples and on down to each of us: "Go into all the world and preach the gospel to all creation" (Mark 16:15). As we go, God is with us.

Now it is your turn to *go* get into action!

10 Ways to Get Going on God's Adventure for Your Life

1. Go to the art museum to study the great works of art. While you take in the beauty, pray and ask God how you can make the world a more beautiful place.

2. Go get a mentor. Ask a woman at your church to be your spiritual mentor or hire a life coach. Build relationships to discover a business mentor.

3. Go take a class. Write down ten skills you wish you had or want to learn. See if there are free or low-cost classes offered at your local rec department, a church, or local school district or college. Try a few new interests. You can also take a skill at which you're a beginner and make it a goal to master it.

4. Go assertively network. Make it a goal to spend as much time chasing the dream as you will spend living it. Get to know people in the field you are most interested in. The broader the network, the more likely you are to discover someone who inspires you, challenges you, and pushes you forward toward your own goals.

5. Go expand your vision: Make a list of questions you would love God to answer. Try for a hundred! Make it a goal to study the vastness of God. Find books on the names of God, the traits of Christ, and more. The bigger your view of God, the bigger your adventure can be!

6. Go gather a dream team. Invite friends who believe in you and the dream God has placed on your heart to be your

dream team. Share your dreams, ideas, hopes, and goals with these women and ask them to hold you accountable for taking action on them. There's nothing like a little positive peer pressure to propel you forward.

7. Go fill your brain. Listen to inspiring music, talks, sermons, etc. Listen to audio and video messages that will inspire and enrich your vision. Take in quality information from quality people and you can become a quality expert too.

8. Go read blogs and books in your dream field. Have a library of information at your disposal. Collect books, sign up for newsletters, and read blogs from experts in the area your heart is drawn to.

9. Go pray and listen to God—and then do what He asks. As you obey God, He will trust you with bigger assignments, more responsibilities, and bigger dreams and visions to move into reality.

10. Go create something tangible. Make a dream board by creating a collage of pictures, words, and graphic designs that represent your hopes, dreams, wishes, and prayers.

Today, start praying, "God, what do You want for my life?" This book might take you into some new territory. Pray God would make you brave to receive all He has planned for you, your life, your relationships, and your future.

You've probably read about the Wife of Noble Character. She is described in Proverbs 31:10-31. Here are just a few of the verses that describe her:

- She *selects* wool and flax and *works* with eager hands.
- She *gets up* while it is still dark; she *provides* food for her family and portions for her servant girls.
- She *considers* a field and *buys* it; out of her earnings she *plants* a vineyard.

- She *sets* about her work vigorously; her arms are strong for her tasks.

- She *makes* linen garments and *sells* them, and *supplies* the merchants with sashes.

- She *speaks* with wisdom, and faithful instruction is on her tongue.

Do you see a common thread? *Verbs!* She's in action!

Together, one simple skill at a time, let's create your personal staircase to success! Step one: Turn the page. Simple!

The sooner you begin, the sooner you can become!

CHAPTER 2

Becoming Decisive

I love helping women grow in their personal lives and in their leadership skills, so every year I take a group of women to Alaska for a kayak trip. When we are away from all the demands of life, in the wilderness, in a setting that daily displays the beauty and majesty of God, we hear God speak!

One day, we were all in a group paddling, two women in each kayak, near the open bay off the shore of Echo Ranch Christian Camp. A whale surfaced just about a kayak-length in front of us. Now, this is quite the once-in-a-lifetime extraordinary sight! But it is also extremely dangerous—that whale could have tipped us over. In the frigid waters of Alaska, you have about five minutes to get back in your boat and get warm before you die of hypothermia. The theme of the trip was "Take Courage," and we had been reading and discussing my book *Becoming a Brave New Woman*. But just how are you supposed to be brave when a whale surfaces just a few feet from your watercraft?

Naomi, one of the most naturally brave and courageous women I have ever met, said, "A whale! Let's go chase it!" so she paddled forward. In the back of her kayak was Kathy, a homeschool mother who wanted to stay alive to finish raising her children. She was paddling backward, away from the whale. It was the perfect picture of indecision. One pulling forward, one paddling backward...and neither of them going anywhere!

And isn't that the way many of us feel so often? We wonder, *Should I move forward? Should I stay put? Is this God's will? Is it my own voice? Should I pull back or move full-steam ahead?*

God Wants You to Decide

Before we talk about decision-making and the will of God, let me share that God wants you to know the best possible plan for your life. Some of you might have sat in a philosophy class where you learned that a Creator made the world, wound it up like a clock, and walked away. But that is not the God of the Bible. God is not aloof. He doesn't just abandon us in our decisions; He longs to give insight and advice to help us make wise decisions.

Early in my Christian walk I learned God's "phone number." Jeremiah 33:3 says, "Call to me and I will answer you and tell you great and unsearchable things you do not know." And God has special promises for those who call on Him.

> Who, then, are those who fear the LORD? He will instruct them in the ways they should choose (Psalm 25:12).

> I will instruct you and teach you in the way you should go; I will counsel you with my loving eye on you (Psalm 32:8).

God cares what you choose and how you choose.
Complex choices can be simplified when made God's
way, in God's timing, and with God's help.

We will jump into some of the basics of knowing what God's will is in a few moments, but for now, be comforted. God does want you to know the best plan for your life and He is committed to helping you discover it.

Think of decision-making as the skill of opening and closing doors or gates. Often we feel like we are on a game show where the host says, "Do you want door number one, two, or three?" The host might show a glimpse of what is behind the door, but not the entire prize. Life feels a little confusing like that, but it is more than just a roll of the dice. The events of our lives are more than just chance. God created us with a free will, wanting us to grow, mature, and learn to make wise decisions.

Unfortunately, some of us might have had "helicopter parents" who decided everything for us and rarely let us solve problems for ourselves. Here are a few helicopter parent overreaches:

- Infiltrating not only your child's play dates as a toddler, but also actual dates as an adult, to make sure he doesn't get his heart broken by some big, meanie girl.

- Following your 18-year-old off to university and moving into the apartment next door so that you can make sure that his refrigerator is full, his clothes are clean, and no one is mean to him.

- Accompanying your grown child on a job interview. Dressing her, sitting next to her, and answering all questions for her while deflecting any that might make her feel less than perfect, and sharing with the possible future employer how mature and independent your 42-year-old daughter is.

- You might be a helicopter parent if you're so worried about your child's safety you hire a Navy SEAL to be the nanny– to your kid who is old enough to be a SEAL![1]

The term "helicopter parent" was originally coined by college admissions personnel when they noticed a change in parents of prospective students. These parents would call the admissions office and try to intervene in a process that had previously just been between the student and the college. Neil Montgomery is a psychologist at Keene State College who studies this "helicopter" mindset and its outcomes.

"I think what the helicopter parents did is they decided, 'Okay, we know what good parenting looks like, we're just going to ratchet it up to a new level, and our kids are going to be even better,'" Montgomery said. "The problem is, when they ratcheted it up, they went too far, and in fact, caused an expansion of childhood or adolescence." This type of over-parenting might lead to children who are ultimately not ready to leave the nest.[2]

"Parents are sending an unintentional message to their children that they are not competent," says Holly Schiffrin, associate professor of psychology at the University of Mary Washington. "When adult children don't get to practice problem-solving skills, they can't solve these problems in the future."[3]

Fortunately, that was not my case. I was raised on a farm and given great freedom to explore. My mom often rolled the decision-making ball back into my court. The question my mom always asked—one my husband and I repeated over and over to our own kids—was, "So what do you think you should do here? How do you think you should handle this? What do you think the next step might be?"

When helping someone make a decision,
don't tell. Ask.

Ask, "What do you think would be the best course of action next?" Don't just tell them what to do. Allow them to listen for God's voice over your voice.

If you are dealing with helicopter parents in your own life, set a time aside to do something to give honor to them, thank them for all they have done for you then, and express to them something like this:

"Mom and Dad, you have given much to make my life great. You have sacrificed, you have invested, you have parented well. Now I want you to know you are free to relax and enjoy the fruit of all the long hours and the many days of giving to me and for me. I want to own the responsibility of all of my life. (You might list areas where they are still contributing funding or being "overly loving.") I think it is vital that I stand completely on my own two feet with God's help so that in the future, I will be completely prepared to give some of the love and care back to you that you have given to me."

I recommend you give a gift that is symbolic of one of the main character qualities you learned from your mom and dad. You might also decide to write a tribute or a personal letter to each parent, perhaps framed with a favorite photo of the two of you.

One year for Christmas, all our sons were students (two in college, one in high school). Not having money for gifts, each of them wrote me a letter. Bill framed the letters with photos of the boys, and on Christmas morning all four men took me blindfolded to my office. Bill had purchased a special cabinet and each tribute was on a separate shelf. Each son read his letter aloud.

Two things happened that day. First, the boys blessed me. I cried because my sons had fulfilled the promise given to the virtuous woman in Proverbs 31: "Her children arise and call her blessed." Second, I blessed my children. The character I saw in their own words, written on their own initiative, gave me the assurance they could run their own lives. Emotionally I was able to free them to be men, masters over their own lives under God's direction. From that point on, I became more of a consultant giving advice when *asked* (rather than all the time!).

Often honoring and being straightforward with a loving parent is all it takes to help each of you know your roles. Clear communication helps everyone know when you want input and when you prefer to think through things with God alone first. It helps people know the sequence of how you prefer to process a choice.

You might want to review three or four of the best decisions you have made and see if you can discern any patterns on how you made that choice and who you went to for advice and when.

All healthy relationships are defined.

—Bill Farrel

By the end of this book, you will have a better understanding of your decision-making patterns and you will gain some new skills that should positively affect your life. You will be able to keep what is effective and toss out what is unfruitful.

Decide Automatically!

What are some ways to know God's voice? What are some strategic decision-making skills that can help us make solid choices? Let's look at a few decision-making patterns that have proved to be effective in my life and family—and in the majority of successful individuals.

The first skill is to pre-decide, or pre-determine as many choices and decisions as you can. It can prove strategic to pre-decide because it creates more of an assembly line efficiency. For example, Ransom E. Olds created the assembly line in 1901 to mass produce the "horseless carriage." The new approach to putting together automobiles enabled him to increase his factory's output from 425 cars in 1901 to 2,500 in 1902. Henry Ford later improved on Olds's idea by installing conveyor belts. That cut the time of manufacturing a Model T from a day and a half to a mere 90 minutes.

To save time, energy, emotion, and money, automate
some decisions.

➧ "It's a strange paradox because human beings are drawn to choice," said Kathleen Vohs, a marketing professor at the University of Minnesota. "We love having more choices, but at the same time the human psyche is easily overcome by them." Whether good or bad, small or large, she explained that the very act of deciding seems to steal away brain power for sticking to goals.[4] Locking in some decisions will save time and effort, keeping you from a constant state of deciding.

Dr. Oz, prolific author, surgeon, and TV show host, obviously has a very full plate of responsibilities and decisions. To lower his stress he eats the same thing for breakfast every morning. In his book *YOU on a Diet*, he says the best way to start is to automate the meal you rush through most. "Make sure the meal fits into your diet plan—you will only have to do this once. Whatever breakfast you choose, stick to it every single day. You won't have to think about what to eat, agonize over choices or count anything. You have already done the hard part."[5]

Take minor choices and automate them: coffee the same way, breakfast the same style, a daily quiet time with Jesus, an evening walk in the park. I have shaved 30 minutes off my morning routine by simply automating the sequence of how I prepare for my day. For example, the choice to place curlers in my hair, then ready my breakfast, and then have my quiet time assures I will look good and feel good in the least amount of time. I like automating the more routine side of the morning—the shower, hair prep, makeup, breakfast. (Yes, most days at home breakfast is the same. I save "breaking the breakfast routine" for days on the road when the culinary choices are more fun!)

I still prefer a little flexibility in my daily quiet times with God. I want to be sensitive to the leading of the Spirit and spend that time the way He directs, but I've definitely automated the choice to spend time with Jesus before I start my workday.

You can also automate some basic moral choices like "tell the truth," "be kind," and "honor your elders with common courtesies." My husband and sons automatically open doors for their wives, their mom, and all women who will let them. It is automatic. My guess is most of you automatically say, "Thank you" and routinely make your bed when you rise too!

In the past several years since the kids have launched, Bill and I have been travelling for business and ministry about 250 days per year. The process of leaving each week for the airport is really only possible because we have automated so much of what needs to happen to get out the door. The dance of my readying the books, making sure we each have nutritious snacks, securing water bottles, locking doors, and turning off lights is timed perfectly now with Bill readying his coffee (no sugar three creams) and then packing and carrying suitcases and computer bags. We can do it all at 4 a.m. without a word in less than 15 minutes because it is so well delegated and automated!

Right now, make a list of ten choices you can automate:

I can automate:

1. get up - take my pill
2. take shower

4. *have coffee/toast while reading the God's word*

3. *praying first*

5. *finish getting ready for appts or cleaning shopping*

6.

7.

8.

9.

10.

There are many more than ten choices you can automate. As you go through life this week, make a note of what choices can simply become repeating patterns of success.

Life rhythms of automated choices can do two important things. First, they save brain space and help us spend time on what *really* matters. Richard Ryan, a clinical psychologist at the University of Rochester, said, "When you're choosing from things you want to do, there's evidence to suggest it's actually energizing...We add energy when we fulfill basic psychological needs. When I choose to see a loved one, for example, that's an energizing choice. Deciding on one of 20 different lotions in a store? That's a different story."[6] Ask which of your choices are daily and draining and decide to automate as many of those as you can.

Second, automated daily choices form layer upon layer of strength—strength that can move a life forward.

I enjoy vacations in Alaska in part because I am emotionally moved when I survey the vast glacier fields. Without getting too scientific, those glaciers move because all those layers of snow packed together are so heavy. The sheer weight of a thick layer of ice causes the glacier to flow. In 1986, the Hubbard Glacier in Alaska rushed forward more than 30 feet each day across the mouth of Russell Fjord. In only two months, the glacier dammed up water in the fjord and created a lake. A beautiful lake was created by the steady forward movement of snowflake upon snowflake.

Automated decisions are powerful snowflakes in our lives. If you build patterns into your life, you'll have a stronger foundation on which to build character.

Small steps taken consistently add up
in a big way over time.

—Danna Demtre

Decide Speed

President Eisenhower was known for saying, "The urgent decision is usually not the most important." A simple grid was created to help him decide *how* and *when* to make decisions. Many military, business, and corporate leaders use a form of this grid in their daily lives. You may find this unique grid helpful too. As you assess your day and make your to-do list, you can first run the list of decisions through this grid to see which you will actually address immediately and which you will delay to a later time.

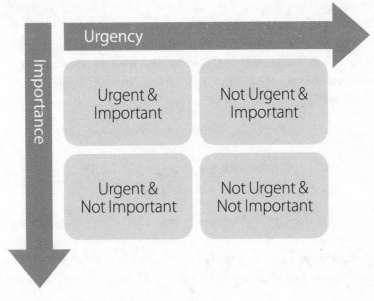

Your choices are:

1. Urgent and important. Do it now!

2. Important but not urgent. Plan ahead and decide when to do it.

3. Urgent but not important. Delegate this task to the appropriate person.

4. Not important and not urgent. Do later. Postpone to your leisure. This is usually a more frivolous issue with little eternal or long-term repercussions.

Decide Your Center

Just as all the planets orbit around the sun, all your decisions will pivot around some core values. People often compliment such surety and confidence in a person by saying things like "She is so centered," "She seems to know where she is going and how to get there," and, "She is such a grounded person."

Strategic decision-making creates focus. I was at a leadership conference and the ballroom was packed to the brim, standing room only. The panel of seasoned leaders was fielding questions and one woman asked Anne Graham Lotz, daughter of renowned evangelist Billy Graham, "Anne, you are wearing so many hats, carrying so many responsibilities. How do you balance it all?" Anne's answer? "I don't."

> Balanced women don't get anything done;
> focused women do.
> —Anne Graham Lotz

Quality decision-making will help you focus, be productive, and accomplish with more efficiency. Centered decision-making gives momentum to your pursuit of God's will. Insufficient decision-making complicates your life and robs you of energy and opportunities.

Notice the priority of decision-making in Deuteronomy 30:19-20:

> This day I call the heavens and the earth as witnesses against
> you that I have set before you life and death, blessings and
> curses. Now choose life, so that you and your children may
> live and that you may love the LORD your God, listen to his
> voice, and hold fast to him. For the LORD is your life, and
> he will give you many years in the land he swore to give to
> your fathers, Abraham, Isaac and Jacob.

God challenged His people to pay attention and make decisions
that protect and enhance life. He knows that life is made up of one vital
decision after another. Every day you are faced with life-and-death decisions, and you must be determined to choose well if you are to avoid
situations that can destroy everything you have worked to establish.

A friend of ours is a police officer and he was sharing a story of cap-
turing an armed violent criminal who pulled a weapon on him. Someone in our small group asked, "How do you get ready for that?" The
captain answered, "You don't get ready. You are ready." Some decisions
are so vital, so important, so far-reaching in their magnitude, you need
to think through them ahead of time. SWAT teams, those serving in
the armed forces, and our protecting agencies are well aware of the
hours and hours of mental training that go into a split-second, life vs.
death decision on the field.

The Watershed

We need skills to discern when the truly monumental decisions are
in front of us. My friend Gari Meacham discusses these vital times in
her book *Watershed Moments* :

> A watershed moment is a turning point brought on by a
> circumstance that stops us in our tracks. Some call it an
> epiphany. A moment when everything changes. A point
> in time when nothing will ever be the same. Like a com-
> pass that provides direction, these are the moments that
> move us to new ways of thinking, relating, discerning, and
> accepting life's challenges.[7]

Some decisions are definitely watershed moments because they define us and the way we view life to the core, the center of our being. As we face those watershed moments and big decisions, it's essential to have a foundational sense of our core life philosophy and calling.

What is your calling as a Christian? The Westminster Catechism tells us, "Man's chief end is to glorify God, and to enjoy him forever." Our goal is to see life and live life from the Creator's point of view. To know God and make Him known.

Jesus seemed to have first expressed a similar sentiment in His prayer to His heavenly Father:

> Righteous Father, though the world does not know you, I know you, and they know that you have sent me. I have made you known to them, and will continue to make you known in order that the love you have for me may be in them and that I myself may be in them (John 17:25-26).

Life Flash

Sometimes it is a routine daily task that reminds us to make a different life-and-death choice. In college, I was driving to a summer Bible conference and my little sister accompanied me. We left very early, before the sun rose, so she was asleep and the car was quiet. I must have shut my eyes just for a moment, but I was jarred wide awake when the driver of an 18-wheel semitruck headed right for me laid on his horn. I had drifted into oncoming traffic and God intervened with a blaring horn to save our lives.

To this day, if I am tired at the wheel, I try to rectify this with sleep, coffee, or exercise—and stopping to rejuvenate. No blinking allowed! The "choose life" principle would also help you decide not to drink and drive, text and drive, or perform any other high-risk activity. Even extreme sports athletes and those in the military and police force train diligently to stay alive while engaging in high-risk activities. They are doing their best to choose life in a world of death.

Other life and death choices, on the surface, seem more convoluted, but they don't need to be. For example, a woman might find herself pregnant and deem the timing difficult or the responsibility of mothering too great. If she takes the "choose life" principle seriously, she will not opt for an abortion. Rather, she will give the baby life and trust that God will provide. Maybe He'll bring changes in her life so she can parent. Maybe He'll send adoptive parents.

I was sitting next to Pam Tebow, mother of Tim Tebow, at an Alternatives Pregnancy Services fund-raiser. I was compelled and inspired as I listened to her story unfold. She shared her harrowingly brave choice: As a pregnant mother of several children, a missionary in the jungles of the Philippines, Pam was told her life was in danger if she carried her child to term. The doctor tried to persuade her to abort her unborn son, but instead, placing his life above her own, she carried this high-risk pregnancy forward. Timmy, as she calls him, was born. And God began to restore her own health as well. Her courageous choice produced one of our nation's most faithful, morally strong young athletes of the decade. Afterward, I told her how inspiring her decision was. She humbly commented that she had a great role model for this kind of love—Jesus, who laid down His life for our own.

Let's put this extremely emotional and politically charged decision in context by hearing from physicians:

Abortion to save the life of the mother is a rare case, a dilemma nearly made obsolete due to the great advancements in medicine. Jasper Williams, Jr., a past president of the National Medical Association, says that, "Doctors now have the tools and the knowledge with which to work so that they can handle almost any disease a patient might have…without interrupting the pregnancy."[8] Physicians on both sides of the debate concur on this, but the strongest evidence may be from a pro-choice physician who said, "The idea of abortion to save the mother's life is something that people cling to because it sounds noble and pure—but medically speaking, it probably doesn't exist. It's a real stretch of our thinking."[9]

The Association of Prolife Physicians explains, "When the life of the mother is truly threatened by her pregnancy, if both lives cannot simultaneously be saved, then saving the mother's life must be the primary aim. If through our careful treatment of the mother's illness the pre-born patient inadvertently dies or is injured, this is tragic and, if unintentional, is not unethical and is consistent with the pro-life ethic."[10]

Often at this point, someone says, "What about if a woman is raped?" While researching my book *10 Questions Kids Ask About Sex*, I discovered a unique set of statistics: The choice for abortion in cases of rape and incest are less than one percent.[11] And in a major study of pregnant rape victims, Dr. Sandra Mahkorn found that 75 to 85 percent did not have abortions. To the victim, an abortion seemed just another form of violence against them.[12]

Let's hear from three women who were the offspring of rape:

Rebecca Wasser-Kiessling, who was conceived in a rape, is rightfully proud of her mother's courage and generosity and wisely reminds us of a fundamental truth that transcends biological paternity: "I believe that God rewarded my birth mother for the suffering she endured, and that I am a gift to her. The serial rapist is not my creator; God is."

Similarly, Julie Makimaa, who works diligently against the perception that abortion is acceptable or even necessary in cases of sexual assault, proclaims, "It doesn't matter how I began. What matters is who I will become."

And my friend Stephanie shares her story in her own words:

> Nineteen-year-old Faye was on what she planned to be her final date with her controlling and intimidating boyfriend. When she told him it was over, things became violent. Rejection wasn't something he was willing to accept and so his rage turned into a brutal rape. Faye's hopes to end a terribly bad relationship turned into the beginning of something much worse. For nine months she carried the constant reminder of that horrific event within her. It was me. I was the reminder. Not just an unplanned pregnancy but a woman's worst nightmare. My birth mom was faced with the pressure to end the life that was conceived so violently. But she understood that a life is a life, regardless of how it began...that while there may be accidental parents there are no accidental people. She started looking

into adoption. How it worked. What she needed to do…I
entered the world with no first name. Just "Baby Salvatore."
But four days later I left the hospital as Stephanie Tyler
in the arms of two wonderful parents who would forever
more be known to me as Mom and Dad.

Stephanie might have started life as the product of a rape, but now
she is the product of a redeeming God! She is equipping mothers
worldwide to be mentor mothers with her M.O.M Initiative ministry.

God even adds an exclamation mark to this good choice to give life
to a child: "Like arrows in the hands of a warrior are children born in
one's youth. Blessed is the man whose quiver is full of them" (Psalm
127:4-5). Every child, every time, is always a blessing. The timing might
not feel like a blessing, but that life *is* a blessing!

God will lead us if we value life—all life. The child with a disability,
the elderly, the mentally challenged…all human life.

The overarching principle is first, choose life.

Since I opened this controversy, the path to healing from the choice
of an abortion is also to choose life. Decide you will not carry the bur-
den alone or stuff the shame and guilt in the deep recesses of your heart.
Choose to bring the pain out in a safe place with safe people, and gain
healing so your life will be filled with light and love.

A friend of mine, the musician Gwen Smith, shares her road back
to life in her book *Broken into Beautiful*. In her life-giving concerts,
she calls women to repent, to no longer hide from their sin but confront it. In doing so you gain the confidence to help others make better choices too. Gwen writes, "What was once a wound has become
a weapon."[13] Thousands of babies have been given life by their mothers because Gwen made the brave decision to acknowledge her sin and
turn from it to the grace and forgiveness of the God who created her
and the unborn child she wishes she could now hold.

Statistically, I know that about one in three readers of this book have had an abortion.[14] That is a number so staggering that I cannot ignore these women in pain, some still wondering what to do to really move forward from this life-altering choice. The majority of Crisis Pregnancy Centers, located in most communities, offer recovery classes, usually free of charge.

Luke 1:79 reminds us that God's plan is "to shine on those living in darkness and in the shadow of death, to guide our feet into the path of peace."

It is in facing the horror of your bad choices
that you gain the power to make better ones.

❡ It was said of Jesus, "In him was life, and that life was the light of all mankind. The light shines in the darkness, and the darkness has not overcome it" (John 1:4-5). The best outcome of a "choose life" attitude is that our hearts remain soft before God and soft toward people. In addition, a "choose life" philosophy helps our minds grow clearer and decisions become more logical and less reactionary. Place yourself on the side of saving the most lives, and your heart will begin to match the God who loved all humankind so much He sent His Son to rescue billions of people.

No matter the circumstance,
when you feel alone in the darkness,
choose life—and light will come.

Value Your Responsibility to Choose Life

I had a watershed moment, an epiphany of sorts, that reminded me how vital it is to be a wise steward or guardian over your own life. It hit home to me in an unusual way and in an unusual place—in prison. Bill and I were invited to speak at a high security prison. The

audience was entirely violent offenders: rapists, armed robbers, mur-
derers, and perpetrators of many other crimes. We were equipping
them with relationship skills because it is often the families who suffer
during a prisoner's incarceration. To help those innocent wives, children, and parents, we helped equip those behind the bars.

As a part of the talk, both Bill and I shared our personal stories.
Beforehand I had prayed, "God, I don't see how these inmates will
relate to my story. Yes, my father drank and he was violent—but at
least I had a dad. God, You need to bridge the gap." But what I didn't
realize was that the gap wasn't all that wide. As I shared about growing
up in a home on the wrong side of the tracks, with a dad who drank
and beat my mom, I saw heads bobbing in agreement—they knew
this familiar pain.

We heard many of the prisoners' stories that day, and for the most
part, there were really only two decisions that separated me from those
sitting shackled before me.

First, I did *not* drink and I did *not* do drugs. I always gave a firm
no, and for the most part, I chose not to hang out with those that did
drugs or drank. I was not a party girl. I saw what addiction did to my
dad and I wanted none of it.

The second decision that placed me at the podium and the prisoners in their jailhouse was an early decision to give my life to Jesus. I
was in God's Word and I decided I would do what the Bible said, not
what peer pressure said. Two choices. Two decisions were all that made
the difference in which side of the electric fence I got to live on. Obeying just a few Bible verses made the difference between freedom and
confinement:

> Do not get drunk on wine, which leads to debauchery.
> Instead, be filled with the Spirit (Ephesians 5:18).
>
> Do not be misled: "Bad company corrupts good character"
> (1 Corinthians 15:33).

In a sense, even the prisoners were fortunate because they still had
their lives. Many who get involved with substance abuse, run with a

rough crowd, and listen to the voices of the foolish instead of the voice of God end up dead.

If you are clear-headed and alert, it is simply easier to make the right choice. Like my momma always told me, "You never will become an alcoholic if you never take that first drink." While I know social drinking, not becoming drunk or controlled by alcohol, is a gray area for many who love Christ, the principle is clear. Sober-minded people make better choices. I have a friend who is a California Highway Patrol Officer. He told me he wished the charts showing how many drinks you can take by weight and still not be legally drunk didn't even exist. He has seen the toxicology reports of those who were not "officially" drunk...but they were "officially" dead.

Be in control of your life,
or someone else will be.

The Oxygen Tanks of Humankind

My grandmother scarred her lungs rushing into a barn on fire to rescue animals. As an elderly woman, she needed her oxygen tank to live—especially to live the more active life she desired. When she had her tank with her, she could even square dance all Saturday night in the arms of my grandfather! The oxygen breathed life into her life. In a similar way, God wants us to breathe life into difficult moments (and sometimes into difficult people!). We should follow in the heart intent of God.

God is a specialist at breathing life
into seemingly hopeless situations.

The God who made the world and everything in it is the
Lord of heaven and earth and does not live in temples built
by human hands. And he is not served by human hands, as

if he needed anything. Rather, he himself gives everyone
life and breath and everything else (Acts 17:24-25).

He wants us to be more like Him, more of a life-giver and hope provider. This "choose life" principle can be extended to apply to all kinds
of situations: the seeming death of a dream, the spiraling downward
of the life of someone you love, a business on the descent. In any situation where it seems that the choices are between death and life, before
you simply throw up your hands in indecision or exasperation, before
you give up, pause and ask…

- What would bring life to this situation?

- What would bring life to this person?

- Who has the skills, talents, time, and energy to resuscitate
  or revive this circumstance?

On Life's High Wire, We All Need a Net!

Have you seen acrobats at the circus walking on the high wire? One
slip, and they fall to their death—unless they have a net.

Everyone needs a net—a support system—to catch them when
they fall. Each person and each couple should surround themselves
with people who breathe life into them, can advise and share wisdom,
and lend their expertise to any given situation. These relationships are
crucial ones to nurture. The Bible says, "Victory is won through many
advisers" (Proverbs 24:6). Insight and wisdom from these key play-
ers will be central to the success of your marriage, your family, and the
home you want to create. Who are some of these net holders and why
do you need them in your life?

Family and Friends

You will grow stronger as you learn to forge relationships with your
friends and family. In a crisis, they will typically be the first ones to show
up. So nurture those relationships during the good times, and if rough
times come, you will have the support you need to make it through.

God promises to honor you as you honor your parents. Much has been written and said on just what it might mean to honor your parents. The word *honor* carries the connotation of ascribing value, showing them respect or recognition that honors them for their worth or role in your life.

Be the kind of person who honors others instead of expecting to be the honoree.

Even in the worst cases, you can choose to honor your parents' position even if you cannot value their personal choices or lifestyle. Your parents gave you life, so that is the starting point. Take it from someone who had a pretty chaotic home: Sometimes the simple choice to be honorable can have the greatest impact. For example, four basic questions guided my choices toward my dysfunctional dad:

- Am I acting toward my father like a healthy daughter would? In other words, from my side of the relationship, am I behaving toward him in a positive manner, not letting his toxic choices lure me into toxic choices? For example, if he yelled, I did not scream in return. He never acknowledged my birthday, but I opted to always call or send a birthday card, usually thanking him for something positive I could think of. I wanted to be a loving person— even if Dad wasn't.

- Am I modeling for my children how I want them to treat me? If I want to be respected as I age, I should show respect to my parents as they age.

- Am I building a strong, healthy, loving life? We honor our parents and grandparents by making good choices with our life—even if they didn't always make good ones.

- Am I imitating Christ when I interact with my parents? Am I loving, caring, and kind? Am I concerned for their eternal and spiritual well-being? Am I building a bridge to his or her heart so I might carry the love of God over the bridge to them?

The verse that motivated me most was Romans 12:21: "Do not be overcome by evil, but overcome evil with good." I know that at the end of all things good will win over evil, and I just like it when good wins a little sooner! (Good girls can finish first!)

The first use of the word *good* in the Bible is at Creation. And that word, *tob* in Hebrew, can also be translated *beautiful*. So in a sense, when in a quandary, I ask: "How can something good, something beautiful, be made out of this situation?"

Spiritual Advisors

Your pastor, friends who are in ministry, marriage and family counselors, small-group leaders, and mentors are some of the people who can play the role of spiritual advisors in your life. You will sometimes face decision points, tough transitions, and difficult circumstances, and you will want people to help you discern God's view on the matter at hand. These key relationships are not made overnight, so the best way to have the spiritual advisors in your life when you most need them is to have them in your life on a regular basis.

Attend church and get to know the pastor (or some of the staff pastors). Join a small-group Bible study. Participate in women's ministries. Involve yourself in parachurch groups that interest you. (Parachurch groups are nonprofit, spiritually based groups that are not a local church. The Fellowship of Christian Athletes, Marriage Encounter, Mothers of Preschoolers, and Moms in Prayer are a few examples.) In a healthy family and friendship circle, family members and friends can play a dual role as spiritual advisors too.

Health Care Professionals

Physicians, allergists, optometrists, nutritionists, OB/GYNs, personal trainers, and other health professionals who care for your physical body are all a part of your success. If you are young and healthy, you may underestimate their influence, but they will become more valuable to you with every passing year.

Professional Experts

You will need insurance agents, financial consultants, legal advisors, mechanics, real estate agents, contractors, and handymen like plumbers, roofers, and heating technicians. People never think they need these people until their house floods, their car breaks down, a computer crashes, a tornado hits, or a family member has an accident. But it is precisely because life is unpredictable and calamities do come that we need to be wise and forward-thinking. You need people who care about you and will give you sound advice on a wide variety of issues.

When life is stable, build friendships with quality professionals so that when the storms of life hit, you will know someone who will hold out an umbrella of shelter and help you weather the storm.

What Are You Looking For?

If you're anything like me, you probably have no idea how your phone works. You're not sure what's really going on in your computer. (You remember it has something to do with binary code...but aren't quite sure what that is.)

As our world becomes more complex, we understand less and less about the objects that surround us. After all, we don't have to know the inner workings of all our machines in order to use them. But when something goes wrong, we place a *lot* of importance on the person who can fix it.[15]

So how do you find these people? Is it effective to do a random Internet search? At times you may discover a quality expert this way, but it is not the most efficient nor the most reliable method. Anyone, including crooks and charlatans, can throw up a website and don fake credentials. The best way to find the kind of top-notch, quality professionals you will need is to know what you are looking for and set a strategy to meet them.

What you want are people you can trust. How can you know that a person is trustworthy? Well, no test is 100 percent foolproof. At any point people can decide to make stupid or selfish choices and leave us in the wake of their sin. For the most part, however, trustworthy people possess the following characteristics.

A Proven Track Record

There are several ways to discern someone's track record:

- Has the company been in business a long time, with few or no reports to their governing board?

- Do they have a solid reputation in the community among leaders and your friends and family?

- If they are new to the field, do they have track records in other areas of service or achievement?

- Have they consistently kept their promises to you and followed through on responsibilities as a life pattern?

- Do they have credentials? In many areas of expertise, professionals can garner certifications, degrees, and authorizations or gain a rating from some governing or business agency. These are evidence of reliability.

- Do they have a clean record?

For the most part, a person's professional record along with some personal recommendations from those you know and trust are sufficient evidence of credibility.

Personal Integrity

- Do they handle their own priorities well?
- Are they trustworthy with money?

- Do they treat their spouses and children with the respect and care they deserve?

- Do they keep their word?

- Do they speak honestly and avoid lying, misleading statements, or manipulation? Do they have a clean record with law enforcement?

- If they did make a mistake or indiscretion, have they owned up to it and paid the fine or penalty?

- Are they willing to do the small things to earn your trust and business?

A Positive Work Ethic

> Don't pay your hard-earned money to people who are not willing to work as hard for their money as you have.

We look for the small things...which end up being hugely important.

- Do they return calls promptly or communicate clearly if there is a delay?

- Do they try to keep a semblance of order in their paperwork?

- Do they give an accurate accounting of hours worked?

Passion

If people's hearts are in their work, they want to do their best because they want to keep doing what they love. We look for people who feel their professions are their callings.

Surround yourself with people who love what they do.

The founder of Logos Bible software, Bob Pritchett, has a growing company filled with enthusiastic, passionate people. He looks for employees whose personal goals dovetail with the company's professional goals. The employees have a lot of freedom to come and go and work in the way they can be most productive. There are not a lot of rules, but there is a whole lot of heart because Bob hires heart.[16]

You can learn how to become confident, brave, and enthusiastic, with a passion for your God-given calling and the skill to build your spark into a roaring fire.

When you surround yourself with the positive,
it is easier to stay positive and choose positively.

Professionalism

Look for those who are successful at what they do or have the earmarks of past success in their lives. Sometimes they are too booked up or too expensive, so go down the list until you find the person who is both personally available to you and a high-quality worker at a rate you can afford.

Look for people who are the best at what they do at a
price you can afford to pay.

People ask us, "Do you use only Christians?" Not always, but shared core values are a priority. If we know a person's faith impacts his or her personal integrity (as it always should) and two candidates have the same professional integrity and proven track records, we will go with the Christian. We want our brothers and sisters in Christ to prosper so we'll often swing business to them. But if the best in the field is not a believer but meets all the other qualifications, we'll go with him or her—unless, of course, we see that person saying or doing something that is in opposition to our faith. Sometimes God uses us to fine-tune the professionals we use and answer their questions of faith as they answer our professional questions in their field of service.

Personal Accountability

Ask your friends, family, and professionals in the field whom they use. Business referrals are a form of accountability or positive peer pressure for the professional. Sometimes we use professionals whom we have helped in their personal lives. The relationship help we provide for a doctor, dentist, or salesperson can be a great motivator to them to do their best for us. You may have an expertise you can share and in being your best, you will meet the best in many fields of expertise. Quality attracts quality.

Let me share a recent example from our family's life that will show how one person can spearhead a support system to breathe new life into a situation. My father-in-law is a brilliant man. He is a retired aerospace engineer who helped design the engines for space shuttles. However, when he was in his forties, he had a stroke that left him partially paralyzed on one side of his body. For years he seemed to adapt and overcome and he functioned quite well. However, as he's aged, a series of severe and exacting health issues piled on, one after another.

Dad's health was deteriorating rapidly and it seemed from all the doctor appointments, frantic middle-of-the-night phone calls, and explanations from health care professionals that the next step was into a permanent nursing facility.

He was so fragile that even a move into a home of any of his kids might prove too stressful and send him nearer death's door. He was extremely frail and unable to care for himself, but due to a loophole in the health care coverage, his provider wouldn't cover a skilled nursing facility unless he fell and broke something—but we all wanted to *prevent* such a trauma! My own husband's health was being undermined as he and his siblings stretched themselves, trying to create a workable plan for the care that would save their father's life.

All of the children live quite a distance from the home they grew up in, so creating a care-giving plan was not an easy task. Each day it became more apparent that Dad needed someone who really cared about his health and could live with him around the clock, at least until a solid long-term plan could be established. The care-giver would need to be able to motivate Dad, would have to be wise enough to handle the difficult and often delicate issues associated with caring for someone too ill to care for himself, and someone strong enough physically to move and carry Dad when necessary—often several times each hour.

In addition, Mom is still in the picture and she was racked with fears. As stranger after stranger came in to care for Dad, her stress was elevated and her emotional health was compromised. Her well-being was a huge consideration. So we all put our heads together and asked, "Who has the skills, the talents, the physical, mental, intellectual and spiritual strength, and engaging, flexible personality to breathe life into this situation?"

We first looked to our extended family because we knew both Mom and Dad would be more comfortable if the caregiver could be someone they already knew.

Our youngest son, a recent graduate from an engineering program, had three weeks available to use before moving to another state for his master's program. Caleb went to university on a football scholarship, so we knew he was strong. He'd built a home on the mission field so quickly and accurately that his teammates nicknamed him "The Machine," so we knew he was intelligent and capable. Caleb and Dad shared much in common. They already had a good friendship (due to the fact that they might be the two smartest men in the room at any family reunion). In addition, our son Caleb is immensely compassionate and patient. He is also a bulldog of persistence when it comes to solving problems. He will outlast any obstacle until victory is garnered!

Caleb readily agreed to be the temporary caregiver. He moved in, was trained by all the health care professionals, and began to rehab his grandfather. In addition, those two engineers redesigned doorways and gates, a patio, a desk, and a wheelchair to make them more user-friendly for Dad. Caleb is such a workhorse that when he wasn't caring for Grandpa, he rebuilt the patio, a ramp, a gate, and several other areas of their home to help give Dad independence and access. Caleb was a coach and therapist extraordinaire. Two weeks after he moved in, Dad was stronger mentally and physically than we had seen him in several decades. The change was nothing short of a miracle. Caleb breathed vibrant life into the situation!

When you have suffered a setback, experienced a grave loss, when you are struggling with depression, hopelessness, uncertainty, or overwhelming grief or discouragement, ask, "Who or what could breathe life into me and this situation?"

Choose to Value Your Life

Your life is precious too. God gave you life:

> So God created mankind in his own image, in the image of God he created them; male and female he created them...God saw all that he had made, and it was very good. (Genesis 1:27,31).

> The Lord God formed a man from the dust of the ground and breathed into his nostrils the breath of life, and the man became a living being (Genesis 2:7).

> For you created my inmost being; you knit me together in my mother's womb. I praise you because I am fearfully and wonderfully made; your works are wonderful, I know that full well (Psalm 139:13-14).

Catch that? God created people and said His creation of life was very good! Remember, this word *good* also means *beautiful*! You are "fearfully and wonderfully made!" Are you feeling good about yourself yet?

To God, His creation is of upmost value!

> You are valuable, priceless, treasured,
> cherished, and prized by your Maker.
> Live like you believe it!

As author Max Lucado emphasizes, "If God had a refrigerator, your picture would be on it. If He had a wallet, your photo would be in it. He sends you flowers every spring and a sunrise every morning...Face it, friend. He is crazy about you!"

When a decision needs to be made, the first thing to consider is how to value human life—including your own life! In the book of Esther, Israel was on the brink of genocide because of an evil leader. Queen Esther's cousin pointed out that God had made her queen for a reason. Maybe, like Esther, you've come to the point of making this decision "for such a time as this!" (Esther 4:14).

> When at a fork in the road, pause to ponder,
> "Why would God place me right here, right now?"

Remember: Right choices will bring the right results!

CHAPTER 3

Becoming Wiser

A woman was climbing a tree when suddenly she slipped. She grabbed a branch and was hanging there. After an hour or so passed, she was feeling exhausted. She looked up to the heavens and cried out, "God, help me—please help me!"

Suddenly the clouds parted and a deep voice resounded, "Let go!"

The woman paused and looked up at heaven once more. She said, "Is there anyone else up there?"

We all struggle to hear the voice of God and walk in step with His plan for our lives. And we wrestle with letting go and trusting that we have heard from God. That's why we look for ways to listen for the heartbeat of God for our life. We only get one life, and if you are like me, you want to squeeze out of life all the best God has for you. I want to get it right...and so do you!

When I am at a fork in the road,
I ask God what the next step is, and He leads with a verse.
His Word is a whisper to my soul, a light to my step,
and a strong arm around my shoulder.

In the front of my leather covered Bible, I've written verses God gave to me along life's path when I have asked for confirmation on the next step.

⁹ When I was asking God if I should marry Bill: "Take delight in the Lord; and he will give you the desires of your heart. Commit your way to the Lord; trust in him and he will do this. He will make your righteous reward shine like the dawn" (Psalm 37:4-6).

When asking what my new role in ministry should be: "For I have not hesitated to proclaim to you the whole will of God" (Acts 20:27).

When I had to move from a city I loved and the home Bill had built for me for a new ministry job for Bill: "Everyone who has left houses or brothers or sisters or father or mother or wife or children or fields for my sake will receive a hundred times as much and will inherit eternal life" (Matthew 19:29).

When asking the best use of my college degree: "On my account you will be brought before governors and kings as witnesses to them and to the Gentiles…Do not worry about what to say or how to say it. At that time you will be given what to say" (Matthew 10:18-19).

When asking how Bill and I could best work together: "My mouth will speak words of wisdom; the meditation of my heart will give you understanding" (Psalm 49:3).

These are just a few of the most vital verses God gave me at those significant turning points of life. I needed God's wisdom to intersect with my path—and God gave wisdom. God wants to lead you. He wants you to have wisdom. I think the struggle always comes in wondering, "Is this my will or God's will?"

I have four simple principles or processes I walk through immediately when I am wondering what the next step might be.

I Seek Counsel

● Go to the Word and investigate what the Bible has to say on the subject. Ask God for direction, and when He gives you a verse—record it! This way, if things get tough, you can go back and see that God gave you clear counsel.

Seek for your heart to match God's heart.

Also go to counselors. Spend time with those who love you, love God's Word, and love helping you find God's will. Mentors, Christian counselors, parents, grandparents, teachers, professors, Bible study leaders, and clergy are some who would easily be comfortable helping you discern God's will.

I Listen for the Spirit's Conviction

When you go to Bible college, you learn how to exposit (rightly divide) God's Word. One of those principles is that if it is important to God, God will repeat Himself. I have found that true in my life too. When God is trying to get my attention, I hear the same message from all different sources—in my quiet time, in a sermon, in the lyrics of a song, on the radio, in a book, in a magazine or blog I might be reading, or even from the lips of a friend.

I also look for the fruit of the Spirit as I step forward on a decision. Sometimes God commands us to take a step in the direction He is leading and then He opens the path of provision. In Joshua 3, the priests are carrying the Ark of the Covenant over the Jordan River into the Promised Land. The Bible says that *as soon as* their feet touched the river, the water stopped flowing. Not before.

Sometimes you have to step out in faith and look for the fruit of the Spirit. If you're stepping into God's plan, you will feel and see "love, joy, peace, forbearance, kindness, goodness, faithfulness, gentleness and self-control" in your life (Galatians 5:22-23).

I Ask for Confirmation

If God can work with a man of little faith who threw out a fleece, God can send me a sign, a nudge, a whisper—or what sometimes feels like a whack from a 2 x 4!

So what do I mean by a fleece or a sign? Let's look at the life of a timid leader. Can you relate to being a little intimidated when you are put in charge and people are looking to you for direction?

We can learn a lot from Gideon. God had assured him that if he went into battle for the noble cause He had directed, Gideon would win the battle. But Gideon was afraid. It was war, after all, and fear is pretty normal. So he asked God to make Himself clear—very, very clear:

> Gideon said to God, "If you will save Israel by my hand as you have promised—look, I will place a wool fleece on the threshing floor. If there is dew only on the fleece and all the ground is dry, then I will know that you will save Israel by my hand, as you said." And that is what happened. Gideon rose early the next day; he squeezed the fleece and wrung out the dew—a bowlful of water. Then Gideon said to God, "Do not be angry with me. Let me make just one more request. Allow me one more test with the fleece, but this time make the fleece dry and let the ground be covered with dew." That night God did so. Only the fleece was dry; all the ground was covered with dew (Judges 6:36-40).

Some challenges look pretty intimidating and our very patient God knows we sometimes need some extra encouragement. God was very patient with Gideon. He told him not once, not twice, but three times to go into battle—and he would win!

God is kind to send message after message
to confirm our future path—especially if we are
feeling a little freaked out by the challenge!

Let me give a quick example. When we moved into the pastorate we also moved to Southern California. The housing prices escalated $60,000 in six weeks. There was no way we'd qualify for the finances to afford an already-built home. Our only shot at a home was to secure the funds and build it—ourselves!

Bill did have experience working as an architectural draftsman and he was very handy at the remodel on our first home, so we both believed he had the skill. But he also knew the huge time commitment building a home would be. He just couldn't see how he could build a home and build a church family at the same time. The more we looked at housing options, the more we felt we should at least pray for the miracle of a home. So we asked for a fleece. Bill asked God, "Lord, if this is Your will, make it obvious this Sunday at church."

After the service, as people exited, the plumber, the cement worker, the roofer, the cabinet maker, and a contractor all offered to donate time to build a home—and a parishioner offered to help with the down payment!

I Look at the Circumstances

Sometimes all the doors look closed. But Jesus told us this:

> Ask and it will be given to you; seek and you will find; knock and the door will be opened to you. For everyone who asks receives; the one who seeks finds; and to the one who knocks, the door will be opened. Which of you fathers, if your son asks for a fish, will give him a snake instead? Or if he asks for an egg, will give him a scorpion? If you then, though you are evil, know how to give good gifts to your children, how much more will your Father in heaven give the Holy Spirit to those who ask him! (Luke 11:9-13).

Sometimes God wants us to knock on a door for a length of time to build passion in our hearts— the kind of passion that will carry us forward once the door has been opened by God.

Eventually, if it is God's will, the doors will open. The ducks will line up. The dominos will fall. The pieces of the puzzle will form a beautiful picture of your future!

But we are human. We are fallible. Our motives can be muddy, our thinking cloudy, our emotions confusing. God's leading can be very clear, but in our humanity we doubt, we wonder, we question. This is why having some tests we can run on our decisions helps make us wiser and leads us on wisdom's path. Think of these tests like the virus scans you run on your computer—they help keep out the bugs!

Test It!

Bill and I have developed some ways to test decisions to give clarity and confidence that we are proceeding prudently, sensibly, and confidently. Years ago, when Bill was early in his role as a lead pastor, he noted the large number of people who struggled with basic life skills, including the tension of decision-making. He created several tests, or grids, people could use to make decisions wisely, carefully, and reasonably.

Bill says, "The most common method for making decisions is to do so by instinct. You are faced with a decision. Your instincts kick into gear based upon your life experience and your emotional programming. A decision 'occurs' to you that feels right. In the absence of any other decisions that seem better, you commit to this course of action."

Frank Crane comments on the drawbacks of this accidental approach to decision-making: "Most of the things we decide are not what we know to be the best. We say yes, merely because we are driven into a corner and must say something."

Bill continues: "If the emotional programming of your life is healthy, these natural decisions can be strong and effective. If, however, the emotional programming is flawed or underdeveloped, these natural decisions are generally short-sighted and lead to complicated results."[1]

Most people have some family dysfunction in their background. We should at least pause to ask, "Am I functioning by feelings—my inner gut instinct?" In healthy decision-making, feelings follow decisions. They do not steer them.

My husband often wisely reminds those he coaches, "If you make decisions accidently, don't be surprised if your life becomes an accident."

If your home was healthy, your instincts are more trustworthy and these reactive, knee-jerk decisions might be generally healthy; however, if your home was dysfunctional, then your decision-making instincts will also be dysfunctional. Most of us come from less-than-perfect home environments, so we need to train our instincts by learning healthy decision-making tools and using them over and over until the learned becomes the natural.

The more you think through your choices, the more you train your inner instincts to be healthy and wise. This means as you age, if you follow the path of testing choices, you *will* become wiser and your inner voice will become more trustworthy.

You Can Decide to Do Differently

I've already shared that my own home of origin was chaotic. I am the firstborn daughter of an alcoholic father with severe rage issues. My dad had a broken heart, and to numb the pain, he drank. When he felt bad about himself or his life, he raged at others. Because of my father's unpredictable behavior, my mother was controlled by feelings of fear and helplessness. Five of every seven days a week my dad traveled, and my mother struggled to get some normalcy in our lives. Then the weekend would come and we would all wonder if we would make it out alive. My dad was suicidal, out of control in his choices and behaviors, and abusive to us. Because of this, being the eldest, I felt I needed to control what was obviously a very out-of-control home. I lived with a deep sense of dread and fear. I felt a need to "fix" my home, as if I had the sole responsibility for making things better.

The coping mechanisms that I developed to survive included...

- Perfectionism. *Maybe if I am perfect, life at home will improve.*
- Controlling behavior. *Maybe if I plan every detail, life will improve.*
- Rebellion. *Maybe if I act out, life will improve.*

- Denial. *Maybe if I pretend this isn't happening, life will improve.*
- Overwhelming optimism. *Maybe if I hide from reality, life will improve.*
- Avoidance. *Maybe if I sidestep or evade, I won't have to deal with this and life will improve.*
- Workaholism. *Maybe if I just work longer or harder, life will improve.*

I did survive, and after I began a relationship with Jesus, God has moved me from a survivor to a thriver. However, God had much to unwind and then reteach me in the area of decision-making.

If I just went by my gut reaction, I would have repeated my dad's methods of decision-making: drinking to cover pain or raging if things didn't go my way. Or perhaps I would have repeated my mother's early decision-making patterns, like denial or fear-based choices. Or, unredeemed, I could lapse back into one of the faulty coping mechanisms above.

Do any of those coping mechanisms sound familiar to you? If you're a perfectionist, you overthink decisions and stall in indecision, fearing a mistake. If you exhibit controlling behavior, you feel responsible for making all the decisions, running over people and relationships if necessary. If you're in rebellion, you oppose authority figures regardless of the negative outcomes. If you're in denial, you avoid decisions because you refuse to face reality. If you're an overwhelming optimist, you only look at the positive pieces of a decision rather than the decision in its entirety. If you're an avoider, you refuse to make decisions and try to get away from the stress of deciding. And if you're a workaholic, you only make decisions to look good, gain fame and fortune, or keep up appearances with the pursuit of possessions.

Some of these coping mechanisms are a little healthier than others. As a counselor once said to us, "At least if your coping skill is workaholism, you have the money to pay a good counselor to get healthier!"

Even so, all the faulty coping mechanism patterns have the fatal flaw of being reactions rather than responses. These defective decision-making methods are too emotionally driven—or else so cerebral that emotions are entirely missing. A healthy decision-making method will use your mind to guide your emotions, landing both safely on the shore of a solid answer, one that moves your life forward.

We, however, are not required to make decisions by instinct. We have been equipped with the ability to discern a wise course of action in each decision of our lives. We have been given the mind of Christ (1 Corinthians 2:16), and we can utilize that ability to make effective decisions.

Quality is never an accident;
it is always the result of high intention, sincere effort,
intelligent direction and skillful execution;
it represents the wise choice over many alternatives.

—William Foster

Healthy decisions cause growth in our lives. With each passing year, we are faced with challenges, opportunities, and responsibilities that seemingly are bigger and more demanding than the year before. Healthy decisions move us forward step by step so that each year we are prepared for what comes our way.

The real complications in life come when
our maturity does not match our challenges.
Simplicity will come when our maturity
surpasses our challenges.

We win and the complications of life lose as we mature in our decision-making and coping skills. My husband puts it this way: "I used to think that some people were born with the ability to recognize and pursue healthy decisions while others were doomed to miss strategic decisions or make short-sighted choices. If that were the case, I was sure I had been left out of the group that was born to be strategic. I have since discovered that any time we are faced with a decision, we can perform a number of tests that give guidance, clarity, and confidence to the process."

Decision-Making Skill 1: The Obvious Test

When you are faced with a decision, it's helpful to determine if this is a simple decision or a more complicated choice. Before you put a lot of effort into any decision, ask yourself, "Is this decision so obvious that I am wasting time thinking about it?" The reason these decisions are obvious is that God has already clearly spoken to these areas of life or they are generally accepted as the best practices. If you put too much thought into these decisions, you get needlessly sidetracked and train yourself to stall when you ought to push forward. Consider these obvious decisions based on the best practices in life:

- Get out of bed. Get dressed. Brush your teeth.
- If a police car pulls up behind you and turns its lights on, pull over.
- Get a good night's sleep regularly.
- If someone does something nice, say, "Thank you."

Here are some of the most obvious decisions we face as women that have been clearly directed by the one who made us:

- Input God's Word into your mind in some way every day (Romans 12:2; Psalm 1:1-3).
- Choose what is good over what is evil (Romans 12:9).
- When faced with sexual temptation, run away from it (1 Thessalonians 4:3-8).
- When you want to worry, pray instead (Philippians 4:6-7).
- In the midst of every situation, find a way to give thanks (1 Thessalonians 5:16-18).

- Confess sin as soon as you are aware of it (1 John 1:9). Don't explain it or justify it; confess it.

- Choose your friends wisely (1 Corinthians 15:33).

- If a friend asks you to lie for him, just say no (Colossians 3:9-10).

❧ When you train yourself to do the obvious, you develop habits that become automatic. These habits make you more efficient as they conserve your energy for more complex choices. They also raise your confidence level as success in simple tasks builds a track record of encouragement for the decisions that are not as obvious.

Elisabeth Elliot was a young woman when her husband, Jim, was murdered as a martyr in the jungles, leaving her with an infant daughter. Elisabeth made a "do the obvious" statement when she adopted the simple decision-making principle, "Do the next thing." Love the next person; care for the next need; answer the next call. She moved from a life that was unraveling to a strong, vibrant ministry and personal life by simply doing the next thing.

People often ask, "What is God's will for my life?" The best place to begin is to do the things that are obviously God's will, because God spelled it out just that simply. Ask yourself, *Am I...*

- *Saved?* This is good, and pleases God our Savior, who wants all people to be saved and to come to a knowledge of the truth (1 Timothy 2:3-4).

- *Spirit-filled?* Do not get drunk on wine, which leads to debauchery. Instead, be filled with the Spirit (Ephesians 5:18).

- *Sanctified?* Therefore, I urge you, brothers and sisters, in view of God's mercy, to offer your bodies as a living sacrifice, holy and pleasing to God—this is your true and proper worship. Do not conform to the pattern of this world, but be transformed by the renewing of your mind. Then you will be able to test and approve what God's will is—his good, pleasing and perfect will (Romans 12:1-2).

- *Sexually pure?* It is God's will that you should be sanctified: that you should avoid sexual immorality (1 Thessalonians 4:3).

- *Saying thanks?* Give thanks in all circumstances; for this is God's will for you in Christ Jesus (1 Thessalonians 5:18).

- *Suffering for right?* Those who suffer according to God's will should commit themselves to their faithful Creator and continue to do good (1 Peter 4:19).

- *Seeking God?* Those who seek me find me (Proverbs 8:17).

God moves us from the known to the unknown
when we are already doing His Will.

Do the obvious. Start doing these things that God says are His will for you!

I love Elisabeth Elliot's model. Before I do anything, I pray "God, show me the next right thing."

Let me give you a series of simple examples.

When I was in college, my parents were going through a divorce, so I helped my mother move back to the safety and serenity of her parents' family farm. *That was the next right thing.*

I was already registered for college, so I moved into the dorms when my parents' marriage dissolved and they each moved away from the city we had been living in. I worked hard to get A's in my classes because no one—not my mother, my father, or me—needed any more drama from anyone. And because I didn't know what kind of help I would get economically, I needed to get good grades so I could keep my scholarships. *That was the next right thing.* To guarantee I would have money to live on in this unstable time, I also applied and was hired for two part-time jobs. *That was the next right thing.*

I was a competitive gymnast, so I enrolled in a PE class for gymnastics. A coach noticed my skill and invited me to try out for the diving

team (which had potential for a scholarship). Since there was no gymnastics team at this college, it made sense to at least try out. I made the
team. *That was the next right thing.*

A friend I made on that diving team invited me to a Bible study. I
went and during the prayer at the end of the meeting, the leader gave
those attending the opportunity to commit or recommit their lives
to Jesus. I prayed and recommitted my life to Jesus. *That was the next
right thing.*

The leader invited me to return the next week and bring friends. So
the next Sunday, I went through the entire men's and women's dorm
and invited everyone, and 20 people came with me. *That was the next
right thing.*

It was obvious to the leaders that I had the seeds of leadership in
me, even though I was new to walking in the faith. So Tina, one of the
women leaders, invited me to attend a one-on-one mentoring discipleship appointment with her. I said, "Yes!" *That was the next right thing.*

I committed to coming each week to both the large meeting and
the one-on-one meeting. Then she challenged me to read the Bible
every day. So I did. *That was the next right thing.*

She then upped the challenge to share my faith on campus. So I did
it—every day! *That was the next right thing.*

This created a track record of trust, so she invited me on to the leadership team. I said, "Yes!" *That was the next right thing.*

The leaders were all invited to a leadership conference for more
training. I said "Yes!" *That was the next right thing.*

At that conference the speaker challenged us to consider the call to
full-time ministry. I prayed, "Not my will but Yours, God." *That was
the next right thing.*

At that same conference, after that extended quiet time with God, I
walked into the lobby. When a handsome young man asked me, "What
did God teach you?" I answered him. *That was the next right thing.*

That young man was Bill Farrel. We began dating, and we asked
God to lead our relationship. *That was the next right thing.*

On December 14, 1979, I married Bill. *That was definitely the next
right thing!*

See how a series of smaller wise choices grew into a series of more important right choices? Then those more important choices grew into a few very vital life choices—all by doing "the next right thing." All the big decisions in life are built upon the foundation of *do the next right thing*.

This principle is reflective of Psalm 84:7: "They go from strength to strength, till each appears before God." When you move from right thing to right thing, you move from strength to strength. Doing the next right thing propels your goals, your character, and your life forward.

Two of our sons, both coaches, have seen that if you can help an athlete or a team experience one win, winning gets into their heart, their spirit, their psyche. In other words, winning leads to more winning, and success makes way for more successes. This is called a *winning mindset*, and it is developed win by win. Karch Kiraly, when asked how he prepared to win Olympic gold in volleyball, replied: "I never did. I only prepared to win the next day." One success prepares us to expect, work for, desire, and plan for another success.

Rightly motivated, this is the pattern of excellence often talked about in the Bible. This mindset, under the pure direction of the Holy Spirit, produces a desire to give our best for God…every time.

But you don't need to strive for any trophy. Rather, rest in the assurance that God will honor the outcome of the series of healthy choices. You will become a woman who wants the best for herself and for everyone else too—and you will gain the courage, confidence, and assurance to believe that true success, God's definition of winning, can happen for anyone who wants it.

Speaking in public is seen as one of the most dreaded possible tasks, with most people saying they would rather volunteer for a root canal than give a speech! To get over the anxiety and fear of speaking, I had to take my eyes off myself. I focus on knowing God is true to all of His promises, and if I do my part of preparing well and crafting a speech that is prayed through, thought-out, timed, and audience-focused, I can stand on stage confident that God will show up. I picture the audience each receiving a personal gift from God as I speak; I picture them being appreciative of me and the words God has given me to share. As I picture success, I can relax while on stage. If the speaker is relaxed and enjoying herself, most often the audience relaxes and enjoys the speech too. As audience after audience responds positively, confidence grows.

> A winning mindset keeps my focus
> where it should be: on a faithful God
> and the precious people He longs to love.

> Success is doing your very best and
> leaving the result to God.

Decision-Making Skill 2: The Wisdom Test

Not all decisions are obvious. Most of the decisions we make require some level of discussion, deliberation, and discernment. This is why the Bible puts such a high value on wisdom, which is the ability to apply truth to situations in a skillful and beneficial way.

Most people are not even aware of the vast amounts of information they casually discuss every day. In the smartphones we use every day are computers more powerful than the one that first put men on the moon! Yes, we have vast amounts of knowledge. However, wisdom is much more than knowledge.

> Knowledge is the *what*.
> Wisdom is the *how* and *why*.

Wisdom asks, "How does this apply to me?" "Why would I want to do it?"

The path for developing wisdom is littered with questions. Wise people ask questions with a sincere desire to find answers they can apply to real life. They know they will not get all their questions answered, and they are aware that their questions will change as they gain new insight and adjust to the truth they have applied to life.

James 1:5 challenges all of us: "If any of you lacks wisdom, you should ask God, who gives generously to all without finding fault, and it will be given to you." The word picture here is vibrant. God says if you lack wisdom, if you are feeling you are falling short, being left behind, if you are running a deficit on the wisdom accounting sheet, if your suitcase doesn't have enough wisdom in it, if your life feels incomplete due to a shortfall of wisdom, then *ask*. Simply ask, believing that God will answer and give you wisdom. God will give you the kind of specialized knowledge and insight that is needed for the next step.

God won't just give you a little wisdom. God gives generously. God gives wisdom like thick frosting on a chocolate cake, like the gooey sweetness on top of a warm cinnamon roll. God lets you lick the beaters and the bowl of wisdom's brownie batter! God heaps on the wisdom. And God gives it without criticizing, reprimanding, or insulting. God gives wisdom, "without reproach," so He'll never say, "What? Didn't you just ask Me for wisdom? Why are you asking again?" God won't do that. God is happy you are asking for wisdom and is happy to give it.

We know He feels this way about those who ask for wisdom. When King Solomon was given the opportunity to ask for anything, he asked God for wisdom. This was God's response:

> Since this is your heart's desire and you have not asked for
> wealth, possessions or honor, nor for the death of your ene-
> mies, and since you have not asked for a long life but for
> wisdom and knowledge to govern my people over whom I
> have made you king, therefore wisdom and knowledge will
> be given you. And I will also give you wealth, possessions
> and honor, such as no king who was before you ever had
> and none after you will have (2 Chronicles 1:11-12).

Yes, ask for wisdom, because when you ask, you gain and you grow. The day you stop asking is the day you stop growing in wisdom.

A wise person asks questions.

● My husband, Bill, one of the wisest people I know, did a study on how the wisest individual ever asked questions to help develop wisdom in others. Here is what he learned.

Jesus asked His followers questions to encourage the development of wisdom. He was interested in guiding His disciples into a deeper understanding of who He was, so He asked, "Who do people say the Son of Man is?" After they answered, He asked, "But what about you? Who do you say I am?" (Matthew 16:13-16). He wanted them to make the issue personal so they would make a decision.

When Jesus encountered two blind men in Matthew 20, He asked them, "What do you want me to do for you?" He had the power to heal them, and He knew He would grant them their miracle, but He wanted them to make a decision. He wanted them to be fully invested in the new lifestyle that would be theirs.

I would never say there is only one reason Jesus asked questions of those in His world, but one of the reasons was certainly to help them develop wisdom so they could apply truth to their lives.

You can apply the Wisdom Test by asking a set of questions when you're faced with a decision. These questions help you apply wisdom to the situation. If you answer *yes* to all of them, it's clear that your decision is based on wisdom and you probably ought to proceed. If you answer *no* to all or most of them, you have more rigorous work to do to figure out the best course of action. The goal is to put in the least amount of effort to arrive at an effective decision. The wisdom test will help you conserve energy on decisions that you already possess the wisdom to make.

If the obvious test does not make your decision clear, ask the following questions:

- Does this decision line up with my convictions?
- Will the people I respect most agree with this decision? Have I asked them?
- Is this decision based on healthy boundaries that will produce self-respect?
- Will this decision cause personal growth in my life?
- Would I encourage my best friends to make this same decision?

Who is the wisest person I know? How would he/she counsel me on this?

Decision-Making Skill 3: The Priority Test

Some decisions in life require more effort to figure out. You've gone through the Obvious Test and the Wisdom Test, but you still need more evidence that you are making the best decision. This happens when…

- The Bible doesn't specifically address the decision before you.
- You have many options to choose from.
- Your two best options are equally attractive to you.
- The decision will affect your life for a long time to come.
- People you respect have differing opinions on how you should proceed.

When this occurs, there are some simple and practical steps you can take.

First, write out your decision in a positive way. In other words, describe what you will do if you say *yes* to this decision. For instance, "I am considering moving my family to Colorado to begin working for a company there that would result in a pay increase." Because a description such as this encourages you to think about momentum in your life, it is better than saying, "I am considering turning down the job offer in Colorado." Whichever way you go with a decision like this, define the direction you will take if you say *yes* to the decision. Take full ownership of your choice and put your heart into it. You want to leave no room for negative thinking.

Second, make a pro/con list. Create two columns on a sheet of paper. On one side, write down the reasons why you ought to take this course of action. On the other side, write down the reasons why this course of action is not a good idea.

Third, prioritize your reasons. The Bible clearly teaches that priorities lead to progress. Psalm 90:12 challenges us, "Teach us to number our days, that we may gain a heart of wisdom." As you prioritize your thinking, wise decisions make themselves known.

I prefer to use an ABC system to prioritize my lists. This means I assign an A to the vital reasons I identify in my list. The supportive reasons get a B. I reserve a C for the reasons I came up with because I'm creative and can come up with ideas that don't really affect the decision. Some people like to rank the reasons by importance (1, 2, 3...), so choose the scheme you are most comfortable with. For the rest of our discussion, I will assume you are using an ABC system.

Fourth, compare the high-priority reasons from both lists. Evaluate the A reasons for saying yes with the A reasons for choosing no. If it is a tie, then move to the B reasons to see if the decision becomes clear. *Don't be fooled by quantity*. It is quite possible that one list will have more reasons than the other, but this is inconsequential. Quantity is no substitute for quality, and decisions such as this require high-quality conclusions. Many people will automatically choose the list that has the largest number of reasons, which creates an accidental environment for success. The list with the most reasons might be the best choice, but it might not. The way to build clarity is to deliberately prioritize the evidence and discipline yourself to focus on the A reasons.

Let's look at one of the most critical decisions Bill and I made under the Priority test microscope. (I will include both our voices and thoughts as it was a decision we carefully weighed out together.) Let's hear from Bill first.

My (Bill's) decision to become a senior pastor in San Diego County was one of the most interesting chapters in my life. I was 29 and idealistic. I wanted nothing more than to fulfill God's will for my life. I was willing to go anywhere and serve in any capacity to follow God's lead. I had a productive interview with one of the members of the church and decided to accept an invitation to preach at one of their services. I went with great anticipation. The service went well, so the decision-making process began. It was the first time I discovered the power of priorities in figuring out a strategic course of action.

We made a list of all the reasons we should say no to this opportunity:

- The building was poorly designed. For someone who started out in college as an architecture major, this could be a constant source of irritation.

- The ceiling of the auditorium was so low that I could hit it from the platform. If I were going to preach in this facility, I could easily hurt my hand if I got too enthusiastic.

- The door from the auditorium to the office was in the middle of the stage. Part of the stage actually had to be removed every Sunday night to open this door.

- The church didn't seem to be relevant to San Diego County. It had the feel of a country church in Kansas rather than a Southern California church. This included everything from the music to the style of dress to the way the landscape was designed and maintained. (Of course there's nothing wrong with country churches, but this one seemed out of place in the area.)

- The leadership of the church was immature. One man was influential but not savvy. He was brash, unsophisticated, and opinionated. People loved him and feared him, and it was clear that everything would need his approval.

- We would be taking a pay cut to work there. I was a youth pastor at a large church with a healthy salary and benefit package. This congregation was smaller than the other church's youth group, and they would not be able to match the salary I had enjoyed.

- It would be harder to own a home in this community because houses cost more and I would be making less. For the time being, due to the age of our children, Pam would be a stay-at-home mother and work part-time from home when able.

- The congregation was relatively uneducated. Less than half the people had college degrees, and I had recently earned my master's degree. I wasn't sure if I was a good fit in this blue-collar church.

- The church was 25 years old and had never grown larger than 200 attendees. I think a church of 200 is a success, but the potential of a church in this densely populated area was much larger. I wasn't sure of the specific factors, but something was holding this church back.

However, there were a few reasons for considering this opportunity:

- San Diego County is a very nice place to live.
- The church had a lot of potential.
- Pam would be completing a university degree and this community had a brand-new college campus just a mile or two from the church.
- We both love university communities for ministry.
- The community would be growing with the new college and businesses, so the potential for the church to grow was also on the horizon.

- We had each made a list of the kind of city, church, and lifestyle in which we thought we could be most effective. We did this separately, after praying and fasting, and then we compared lists. They were almost identical. After we visited the church, we noticed that most of the things on our "dream job" list were available in some form in this location.

- After Pam and I fasted and prayed, we both had a strong sense that God was calling us to this church and our family to this community.

Bill and I had a lot more reasons for saying *no* to this church than saying *yes*. Especially troubling was the economic stress we would feel upon arrival. The *no* list was longer, and we even liked some of the reasons for declining the invitation better than the reasons for accepting it. Had we based this decision on the number of reasons, we would never have moved to San Diego. But before we made this decision, we prioritized each of the reasons, assigning each one an A, B, or C.

We soon reached the conclusion that every reason on the "don't take this opportunity" list was a B priority. Two of the reasons on the "take this opportunity" list were also B's. But the notion that God was calling us seemed clear. As a couple and as a family, this city and church felt like a good fit for us. We knew we would all grow together. This one A priority overshadowed everything else.

The opportunity for me to have a quality university nearly in our backyard was an asterisk on our pro-con list. We had purposefully worked to put Bill through his graduate program, and now we were both firmly convinced it was a strategic time for me to complete my BA. For our family's future, we both needed some diplomas on the wall. There are many communities with colleges, but this one so matched our priorities, our personality, our lifestyle, and our plans for the future. It seemed a great fit!

However, like other life decisions, we went into this opportunity with many questions. Could Bill overcome the obstacles this church presented? Could we help this church reach its potential? Did this group of people even want to reach their potential? Could our family handle this challenge? Would this church ever prosper enough to pay a salary that would allow us to purchase a house?

Of course, these questions did not get fully answered ahead of time. We did our due diligence, but then we had to calculate the risk, step out in faith, and wait to see how it all worked out. Looking back, following the Priorities Test was a smart move.

Right away, God provided some immediate needs. A family in our home megachurch that was launching us gave us half of a down payment on a new car. Another man to whom Bill had ministered made the commitment (without our asking) to send 300 dollars a month, the difference between our old salary and new one, for the first two years. I got scholarships for college costs. We rented, and a man in our new church then loaned us down payment funds on a piece of property we could afford. Together Bill and I, along with volunteers from our church and community, hammered up a home. We got into a home by a miracle plus sweat equity.

The church struggled along for years but eventually grew to be the largest in our community. The real accomplishment, however, was the number of ministries that were launched from that one church. Bill and I started our writing and conference ministry while we served there. That church became a vibrant hub of creativity, accountability, and courageous pursuits. Listening to the answers from the Priorities Test gave God the tools we would use to build the home, the family, the ministry—the life of our dreams. The work was hard, but the fruit was good, sweet, and lasting!

It was in that church that Bill first began to teach on Simple Skills, and that is where God forged the decision-making tests I have shared in this book. It was in that church that I was given great freedom to create ministries, train leaders, and write and teach many of the principles contained in this book (and many of our other 40 books!).

Whether you turn to the right or to the left, your ears will hear a voice behind you, saying, "This is the way; walk in it" (Isaiah 30:21).

It's Your Turn

What decision are you currently facing that needs the priority test? Describe the decision in positive terms and work through the priority test.

The Decision: [write this in a positive, affirmative way]			
Pros		**Cons**	

Now prioritize each side of the list. In the smaller boxes, write A, B, or C for each reason. Compare A priorities to A priorities, B priorities to B priorities, and so on. If you use these decision-making tests, the difficult will be made simpler!

The Rubber Band

Another way to look at this pro/con model is to think of yourself wrapped between two rubber bands, each pulling in opposite directions.[2] One side is pulling you to stay, holding you in place. The other side is pushing you to change. By writing out the list as a holding you/pulling you comparison, you might gain confirmation on your *Priorities Test*.

Pulling You to Hold Steady

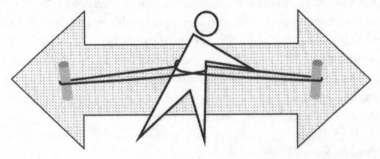

Pushing You to Change Directions

The Decision: [write this in a positive, affirmative way]	
Pulling You to Hold Steady	**Pushing You to Change Directions**

Let me give a quick example on when this pull-push model helped us make a decision on where to live. We had launched all of our children. They were all in college, married, or settled into their own lives and careers. Bill had just transitioned from working as the small groups pastor for Dr. David Jeremiah. Our Love-Wise ministry was expanding; our opportunities for speaking and writing were escalating.

Then the global economic crash came. We didn't see the effects right away because speaking is booked usually a year or more out, but we saw the writing on the wall. Belts were going to need tightening. We'd need all our creativity to weather the unpredictable financial whirlwind ahead. We live in California and we pay what we affectionately call "sunshine tax." (It is not a real tax, but the cost of living is a higher here.)

We decided the world was a blank canvas. Because so much of our work is digital, and we travel to speak anyway, we could live anywhere. So we wondered, "Is God asking us to move?"

First we applied the Obvious Test. We reviewed a few verses we thought appropriate:

> The one who is unwilling to work shall not eat (2 Thessa-lonians 3:10).

We needed to work, so where could we best fulfill this?

We needed to consider whether our aging parents needed care. Was it time to move nearer to them (or move them nearer to us)?

> He must manage his own family well and see that his chil-dren obey him, and he must do so in a manner worthy of full respect. (If anyone does not know how to manage his own family, how can he take care of God's church?) (1 Tim-othy 3:4-5).

> But if a widow has children or grandchildren, these should learn first of all to put their religion into practice by car-ing for their own family and so repaying their parents and grandparents, for this is pleasing to God (1 Timothy 5:4).

There was nothing obvious. Our parents were in relatively good health. We had a conversation with each side, but none of them seemed to need a change. Next, we ran the Priority Test. We asked some friends, family members, and colleagues to weigh in. The opinions on "where's best" were all over the globe! And when we answered the questions from the list above, these were the top priorities:

- Continue a ministry.

- Stay as healthy as possible so we can continue the rigors of a traveling ministry (so a place with good weather looked more promising).

- Have a team around us for help and accountability (again, this could happen most anywhere).

So we weighed out the options and this pull and push approach really helped us know what to do. We set up a rubric, and made a list of top qualities needed in the city that would be the best "home" for us and our ministry. In the end, the list looked like this:

Pulling You to Hold Steady	Pushing You to Change Directions
Major airport within a 20-minute drive	Major airport
Country-like setting (neighbors not too close)	Country-like setting
Zoning to allow us to work from home	Zoning to allow us to work from home
Weather that allows us to be active and healthy	Team of staff and friends to help
Weather that gives our ministry freedom (no snow/ice days)	Church that values our involvement
Housing market to enable sale of home with enough to buy again	Possibly a lake
Team of staff and friends to help with ministry	Living closer to the kids and grandkids
Church that values our involvement	
The ocean	
Kids and grandkids want us to stay near the beach	
Our built-in office and film studio are completed and paid for	

Because we love family we did feel a strong push, but our sons lived in three different states (two were in college and hadn't settled into careers, and the city our eldest lived in put my health at risk). While a few cities did provide the affordable plane ticket a major airport gave, only a few were in climates that were conducive to frequent travel without delays and cancellations, and fewer still had temperatures or altitudes that provided the wellness and health priority we felt we needed in life's second half. We have friends and ministry colleagues around the world, so we knew we could rebuild or hire a staff and team, but trust takes time and at this critical juncture, only a couple of options were very certain. There are thousands of great churches and wonderful pastors who would welcome what we had to give, so for the most part, this was a secondary item (a "B" priority). The housing sales market was mushy and when we crunched the numbers, we knew we would not make the kind of profit that was prudent as we transitioned into full-time entrepreneurial ministry, and even though houses might be more affordable in other cities, unless we made something on our home, a move with a loss this near retirement didn't seem prudent.

Moreover, when our sons and daughters-in-law expressed their desire for us to stay near the beach in case any of them found jobs in Southern California or wanted to use the house for vacations, the pull toward keeping our home and staying put was compelling. So we laid out a "stay put plan" and set a date to reevaluate in the future. At any time, God can add new variables and priorities, and God might push our hearts to another location, but for now God has pulled our heart home. We are staying put in Southern California.

I Just Can't Figure This One Out!

The vast majority of decisions in your life can be figured out using the *Obvious Test*, the *Wisdom Test*, and the *Priority Test*. Every once in a while, though, you will encounter decisions that are elusive. This happens when choices present themselves that are truly different from decisions you have encountered in the past. You are not sure how to get started because you are into new territory with new implications. You may have little life experience to draw on, or no track record to look back on. In order to tackle these decisions, you need to open yourself up to new possibilities.

Decision-Making Skill 4: The Brainstorm Test

This test can be strenuous so you don't want to rely on it often, but there are times when it is necessary to answer the question, "Have I considered every possible solution I can imagine?" One of our great privileges in life is to exercise our creativity. The creativity to identify and explore brand new possibilities resides in all of us because we have the mind of Christ and we are made in the image of a creative God.

To release this creativity we need to open up our thinking. Most of us have developed either discipline or hesitancy in our thinking. We discipline our thinking so we keep focus on the important responsibilities of life. We hesitate in our thinking because of past mistakes or fear of letting unhealthy desires take over. We need to get beyond these barriers when truly new solutions are necessary. Brainstorming can help open up new ways of looking at life.

Here are some steps to unleash this creativity.

Step 1: Brainstorm a solution list.

Write down every possible solution you can imagine. Include ideas that seem ridiculous, absurd, and impossible. It is vital during this process that you do not analyze any of these ideas. The brainstorming process is designed to break through the barriers that have developed during your journey in life. If you analyze or evaluate ideas during the brainstorming process, you will eliminate ideas that could lead to new solutions. The goal here is to get as many ideas on paper as you possibly can in hopes that a new possibility surfaces. If you have difficulty making a large enough list, ask trusted friends, family, colleagues, mentors, or a counselor or other expert in the field to add their ideas.

Do not rush this step. You may want to take breaks and come back to your list a number of times in order to consider the greatest number of ideas. Once the brainstorm list is completed, set it aside for a time. This break can last from a few minutes to a few days. The goal of this break is to shift from a brainstorming mentality to an evaluation mentality.

Step 2: Eliminate the ridiculous ideas.

Cross out any ideas that are truly ridiculous. Be careful not to eliminate ideas that feel ridiculous to you but are actually good possibilities. Again, you may want to ask others to help you figure this out. You allowed these ridiculous ideas to appear on your list to expand your creativity. Now it's time to eliminate them so they don't create clutter as you move forward.

Step 3: Eliminate ideas you are clearly not ready to consider.

Some ideas on your list may sound possible, but you know in your heart you would never implement them. These ideas may not match your personality, your values, or your maturity level. Be careful that you do not eliminate these simply based on your emotional reaction to them. Real change is hard and makes you uncomfortable, so you want to keep challenging ideas on your list. You want to give yourself the freedom, however, to get rid of ideas that you are confident would make you miserable. For instance, I do not have the personality of an accountant. There are many accounting positions I can imagine putting on my brainstorming list if I were considering a career change, but at this point I would eliminate most of these because accounting is not something I am passionate about or skilled at. Accounting would wear me out—and drive the people around me crazy!

The ideas you want to eliminate in this step are those that you know in your heart you would never focus on well enough to succeed. You do not want to commit yourself to a course of failure. It is wise to have someone you trust help you work through this step so you don't get rid of ideas that scare you but could lead to success if you pursued them. Since your trusted friends are not afraid of the same things you are, they often have sharper insight into new possibilities for you.

Step 4: Walk the best ideas from your brainstorm list through the Priorities Test.

Once you have refined your brainstorm list, you will be left with one or more new courses of action. You now need to evaluate these ideas. Since you would do this much work only for a life-changing decision, you want to give this process the focus and time it deserves. If you have more than one idea to pursue, work the process until you have two options remaining. Then create a list for each idea. List the pros and cons for each, prioritize the reasons, and focus your evaluation on the high-priority reasons.

These tests produce a system of decision-making where the majority of decisions can be made expediently and confidently, and the most puzzling can be made with diligence so a solution becomes evident. Be assured, God wants you to know His will even more than you want to know it. God will speak; it is your job to listen. You are a decision-maker and you can figure out the journey ahead with God's good hand on you. We will be able to say, as Ezra rejoiced as he led a nation to rebuild, "Because the hand of the LORD my God was on me, I took courage" (Ezra 7:28).

Test your decisions and then do the next right thing.

CHAPTER 4

Becoming Reliable

No one likes to feel like a flake, a failure, or a fake. Don't we all want to look in the mirror and like the woman we see?

"Thanks, I can always count on you!"

"You are amazing—so dependable!"

"You consistently perform above the rest!"

"You seem so calm, so poised, so together."

Comments like this feel so good to the soul! Becoming a woman others see as reliable, consistent, and trustworthy requires more than tossing about some nice words of affirmation—it is about *earning* those kudos, compliments, and kind words!

In the heart of a reliable woman is integrity—a deep-down desire to live in accordance with the way you were designed by your Creator.

Integrity Matters

To be a woman of integrity means to be complete, upright, and blameless. A woman of integrity holds on to her moral values no matter what peer pressure, the media, popular opinion, or her favorite politician or celebrity says. A woman of integrity refuses to be a chameleon;

instead, she pursues authenticity and uprightness. It is her dependable character that makes her stand out from the crowd.

We all long to live a blessed life. We long for "the gracious hand of our God [to be] on us" (Ezra 8:18). Over 700 times in the Bible we read about God's *anointing*—a word often used to describe how God selects His leaders and royalty—and we want some of that anointing on our lives too.

The Psalmist said, "Surely, LORD, you bless the righteous; you surround them with your favor as with a shield" (Psalm 5:12). We desire God's goodness, favor, and anointing to be wrapped around us and our lives.

In a world that often seems unpredictable, unstable, unkind we long for unfailing love. That craving for intimacy with God and a life more reflective of heaven was placed in us by our Creator.

We crave beauty. We wish for love and protection. The pains and pressure of life can be penetrating—like pelting sheets of rain in a thunderstorm. Think of the last time you were out in the pouring rain. What did you need to be sheltered from the torrent? An umbrella! With God's umbrella sheltering you, though you live in a world with storms, you are not getting damp and chilled. Instead you are protected and shielded. Any "rain" (those difficult, disappointing, and depressing experiences) that is allowed in must first go through God's loving, divine, sheltering character. God is the windbreaker in life's hurricane. "The name of the LORD is a fortified tower; the righteous run to it and are safe" (Proverbs 18:10).

It seems the natural response to receiving shelter from the storm would be to stay under that umbrella of care—and perhaps get to know the One offering shelter.

When we live under God's umbrella of blessing
life is tranquil.
No matter the storm, God is with us.

Have mercy on me, my God, have mercy on me, for in you
I take refuge. I will take refuge in the shadow of your wings
until the disaster has passed (Psalm 57:1).

The Bible tells us that one of God's names is *Jehovah Shalom*, meaning "the Lord is our peace." In the New Testament, it is said of Christ, "he
himself is our peace" (Ephesians 2:14).

If we walk as God designed, with a heart that wants to please and
obey His principles, He will be our shield, our peace, our shelter, and
our guide.

We tend to see peace as the absence of trouble.
Rather, peace is God's calming presence
in the midst of trouble.

Firm Foundations

When building a home, it is all about the foundation. If the foundation is faulty, the house will fall down. How do we know what is true
so we can build our faith—and our life—on it?

We had the privilege of building a home in the suburbs of San
Diego. If you know anything about earthquakes and fault lines, you
know the great San Andreas fault runs the length of California. To meet
code, our home was built to withstand at least a 6.0 quake. Bill went
above and beyond that code. He put the steel rebar into the concrete
foundation and fixed the steel strappings to the foundations. His extra
time and effort were worth it. At least three sizeable quakes that should
have rocked our home have occurred since we built it. Other homes
were damaged, but ours stood rock solid!

Bill made sure our foundation wouldn't slide and crack. In the same way, if we dig deep into God's Word and model a hunger for truth for the ones we love, all our lives are less likely to slide from the secure and centered foundation.

Think of the process of gleaning truth like panning for gold. Choose to run all beauty, information, education, and opinion through the netting of God's Word. If it is truth congruent with the Word, the truth will remain in your pan, like gold in the tray.

God reveals His truth through the Bible because it is God's love letter—His account of what He wanted us to know. While we might gain intimacy with God through things like art, music, emotional experiences, or the teachings of a leader, that "inspiration" is only Truth if it lines up with God's already-given revelation: the Bible.

We must seek to know God in the way He gave to be known—through His Word.

Some people are tempted to simply pick and choose which verses they like and don't like to suit their ever-changing reality. In cases of cutting and pasting truths to suit each individual's whim or shifting public opinion, this confused state creates a situation where the rule of law means nothing. If there is no ultimate truth, no common shared values, no yielding to laws based on Truth, soon anarchy will break out.

We have historical documentation of multiple times in history when man has elevated himself above Truth. One most vivid is in the book of Judges: "In those days Israel had no king; everyone did as they saw fit" (Judges 17:6).

If there is no ultimate Truth, then law, order, and civil society will soon devolve into chaos. In the same way, if you have no moral Truth guiding your life, then your own life will become chaotic because of the accumulating inconsistencies and contradictions.

Jesus told us He was "the way and the truth and the life" (John 14:6).

Knowing His truth can only make your decision-making clearer and empower you on your journey.

Life without a compass is chaos.

You can build your life on the firm foundation
and infallible truth of the Bible.

God wants us to read, understand, and apply the Bible to our lives. However, just as you took lessons to learn to drive your car, it is prudent to take some time to learn to drive your life through an understanding of Scripture.

A pastor's wife, who is a friend of mine, shared a simple system she learned in college. It's as easy as saying your vowels: A, E, I, O, U:

A—Ask questions. Read the verse and see if you can come up with ten questions to ask of the text.

E—Emphasize. Find definitions for key words; look up meaning of key phrases. (You will need a dictionary, a Bible dictionary, and maybe a Bible Encyclopedia.)

I—In your own words. Rewrite a paraphrase of the verse or at least a piece of the passage in your own words.

O—Other references. Use cross-references and commentaries to lead you to other verses.

U—You! Choose a personal application. The sooner you can apply the verse the better!

A fun way to go deeper is to "dialogue" with the Word of God. Ask God questions about what you read. To help, you can print out entire sections of Scripture in double space form. Mark it up and ask questions, and then research to find the answers to those questions. Below is a small example. Simply ask:

Who: Who wrote it, to whom?

What: What is the context of this story? What is going on before and after this passage?

When: When did it take place in history? Are there some things I need to know about in the culture?

Where: Can I find it on a map?

Why: What was the writer's motivation? Is this a teaching passage? A poem that shares a feeling? A story that illustrates a point?

How: How does this apply to life today?

Relish Revival

Yielding to Truth and God's Spirit whispering to your heart is the path to revival, regeneration, and real authenticity. Authentic renewal has repentance at its core. Nothing is more refreshing than a genuine ownership of one's sins against God and His plan for your life.

> Then I acknowledged my sin to you
> and did not cover up my iniquity.
> I said, "I will confess
> my transgressions to the LORD."
> And you forgave
> the guilt of my sin
> (Psalm 32:5).

If you've seen a body in a coffin, you know that a dead person has no reactions. You could talk loudly, slam the door, or poke the body with a pin, and it wouldn't react at all. That is how we are supposed to act toward sin now that we are alive to Christ. In Romans 6:11, Paul reminds us, "Count yourselves dead to sin but alive to God in Christ Jesus."

A person yielding to righteousness, a woman alive to God, acts dead to sin. We refuse to hear, feel, or acknowledge sin. Instead we listen to and react to God's voice and call.

Plant and Water

When we PLANT and WATER the seed of God's Word in our heart, the Holy Spirit has something to work with to get our attention if we are veering off course.

First, PLANT God's Word into your life consistently:

Probe. This is the process of studying God's Word so it makes sense to us.

Listen. Hearing other people teach the Bible and relate how it is affecting their lives encourages growth in all of us.

Acquaint yourself. There is no substitute for reading God's Word consistently.

Nail it down. Memorizing specific verses makes them readily accessible when we need them most.

Think it over. Asking questions like, "How do I live this out? And how does this apply to my life?" energizes God's Word in our lives.

Second, WATER your relationship with God through interactive prayer:

Wait for God. Listen in prayer by saying, "God, You go first."

Acknowledge your sin to God. Confess your sins and receive His forgiveness.

Thank God. Praise Him for the blessings He's given you.

Exalt God. Worship Him.

Request of God. Tell Him your needs.

I practice PLANTing and WATERing God's Word in my life on a regular basis because I know that I am just as susceptible to getting off track as the next person if I don't keep up that daily input of Truth. I have seen this verse rescue me from myself on numerous occasions:

"I have hidden your word in my heart that I might not sin against you" (Psalm 119:11).

Just recently, Bill and I found ourselves off rhythm with each other. I was frustrated by the many tasks still remaining on Bill's to-do list that I thought should have been checked off. In short, I was afraid he would let me down.

There had been an underlying cooling of the temperature of our relationship over a few days, and I began to pray that God would show me who needed to change and own the issue. I secretly hoped it would be Bill so I'd get a heartfelt apology. I could then valiantly forgive him, and I wouldn't have to change my to-do list for him!

I often listen to an audio version of the Bible when I'm at the gym. That day I heard, piped into my headphones, some wonderfully irritating insight. Ephesians 4:1-3 was dramatically read into my heart: "As a prisoner for the Lord, then, I urge you to live a life worthy of the calling you have received. Be completely humble and gentle; be patient, bearing with one another in love. Make every effort to keep the unity of the Spirit through the bond of peace."

God's Spirit gently asked me, *Have you been humble toward Bill or have you already decided it has to be Bill's fault? Have you been gentle? Patient? Have you been bearing with him and all the pile of responsibilities on his list coming from all different directions? When was the last time you said thank you instead of barking out orders or e-mailing requests for action? Pam, have you made every effort to bless Bill? Every effort to encourage Bill? Every effort to lower his stress? Every effort to meet his emotional needs? You are a relationship specialist, so you know better. Have you really been living worthy of your calling? Pam, pause for a moment, right here in this gym, and pray. Ask Me what you can do for Bill that will help him feel My love, My plan, My hope. The way to your hope, Pam, is to meet Bill's needs right now rather than have him meet yours.*

Fortunately, I decided to put into action the message that God had been speaking into my heart. I called Bill up, took him to his favorite coffeehouse, and apologized. I told him the story of how God's Spirit had instructed me, and then I listed off all the traits of his I appreciated but had been taking for granted.

Relational reconnection happened almost instantaneously. Because I was in the Word, the Word was in me, working to renovate me. If we are in the Truth, the Truth can teach and transform us before, during, and after our botch-up.

Keeping in a Right Relationship with God

Have you ever been walking along on a crowded street with someone you love, hand in hand or arm in arm, when the person you are with just stops talking and drops your hand? Suddenly you realize you can't even see him anymore. He has been distracted by someone or something else. How are you feeling? A little slighted? Hurt feelings? Maybe a little panicked or worried? Angry that someone or something else has taken priority over you?

Maybe that's a little bit like the way God feels when we stop walking in step with Him. When we lose sight of Jesus, we are prone to distraction, discouragement, disillusionment, or disobedience.

> God didn't stop walking with us;
> we stopped walking with God.

A life can unravel quickly when you fall out of step with God and the plan He has for you. So how can we minimize the damage to our lives by getting back in step quickly?

Spiritual breathing (exhaling the impure and inhaling the pure) is an exercise in faith that enables you to continue to experience God's love and forgiveness. I first learned this powerful concept from the founder of Campus Crusade for Christ, Bill Bright.

First, exhale. Confess your sin. Agree with God concerning it and thank Him for His forgiveness of it. Confession involves repentance—a change in attitude and action.

Second, inhale. Surrender the control of your life to Christ and receive the fullness of the Holy Spirit by faith. Trust that He now directs and empowers you according to His promises.

> Simple: Breathe out the bad;
> breathe in the good.

Blessed is the one whose transgressions are forgiven, whose sins are covered. Blessed is the one whose sin the LORD does not count against them and in whose spirit is no deceit (Psalm 32:1).

Embrace Excellence

If you want excellence, embrace what is best so your life will be blessed.

So often we might think, *How close can I get to sin without getting burned?* That is the wrong question. The right question is, "How close can I get to Jesus?" When I am near to the heart of God, I am near to the heartbeat of the plan God has for my life. First Corinthians 10:23 sums it up well: "'I have the right to do anything,' you say—but not everything is beneficial. 'I have the right to do anything'—but not everything is constructive."

In Christ, you are free—but what will you do with that freedom? I want to embrace excellence. I want what edifies. Before I say or do anything, I ask, "Will this build up my life? Will it build up another's life? Will this strengthen my marriage, my mind, my relationships, my family, my friendships?"

I don't want to waste any of my time or God's time on anything that isn't making someone's world better.

Excellent in God's Image

Excellence isn't something you need to strive to achieve; rather it is an identity you embrace. You were made in the image of God. Act like it! At the end of each day, ask yourself, "How have I imaged God today?"

As we hold fast to our identity as a reflection of God's image this motivates us to live in a manner worthy of our calling. When you picture yourself as the daughter of the King of Kings, it is natural to behave as a princess. When we have dignity, it is natural for us to treat others with dignity and honor.

To live as a princess, we should look for ways to interact with the King, our Heavenly Father. In a recent study, it was discovered that the difference between those who live differently from those in the world who do not know God, is simply having at least four meaningful inter-actions with the Bible per week.[1] This includes attending church and small group Bible study, having daily devotional times, and reading God's Word. Where can you weave in time for God's Word daily?

The Word fortifies our lives, our minds, and our relationships. The more of God's Word we have in our lives, the braver, more courageous, more Christ-like we become.

Look for ways to layer God's Word into your life in natural rhythms: as you dress, walk, eat, sleep, drive, and rest. Take Jesus with you on your journey!

Set aside a time each day to PLANT and WATER your life with the Truth of God's Word. If you are looking for a starting point, I find reading a Psalm and a Proverb each day is an easy place to begin. Or begin by reading the story of Jesus's life in Matthew, Mark, Luke, or John.

Just like you would keep an appointment with someone important, like your doctor, pastor, or the President, set an appointment that you plan to keep with the God who created you and wants to strengthen your life and relationships.

God, each day I plan to meet You at:

Time:
Place:
Using tools of:

The place in the Bible I will start having a quiet time (or do next in your current devotional) is:

Being with Christ through His Word will make you more like Christ. You will experience a transformation. You will like the woman you are becoming more and more each day. You won't have to strive; you will simply be renewed and regenerated moment by moment through Christ's power in you.

Place yourself in God's presence.
He will transform you with His power.

One of the positives of integrity is you won't have to keep track of stories you have told or the web of lies you have spun. You can simply be *you*! That is the blessing—looking in the mirror and liking the woman you see there.

Make a Marker of Your Maker

In my home, on my walls, and especially in my home office, I keep reminders of my desire to walk in integrity. In the Old Testament, God called His people to build altars to remind them of everything He'd done for them.

Following in this tradition, I have a few memorials on my desk. A figurine with a beach umbrella as a reminder to stay under God's umbrella of blessing. A heart-shaped paperweight to remind me to seek God with a whole heart and a pure heart. A compass as a reminder to seek God for direction. Photographs of my family and friends to remind me that every choice I make affects those I love as well.

When I am tempted to step out from God's will, out from under the umbrella of blessing, I picture myself having to own up to some sin or failure to all those faces. Those are talks I would rather never have. I would much prefer spending my time pouring positives into those lives instead of unravelling some negative consequence I created by my own selfishness or rebellion.

The last memorial on my desk is a frame filled with Bible verses. Under this glass frame, I see the commands and promises of blessings if I obey. What people don't see are the newspaper and online articles I've placed behind those verses. They're articles about leaders who have spiraled out of control and crashed their lives, ministries, marriages, and children's lives. When I see that frame I say to myself, *Seek to be the blessings on the front not the headlines on the back.*

Bill and I often have the delightful opportunity to meet the children of some of the most beloved Christian leaders you and I hold dear.

When given this opening, after spending a little time getting to know the son or daughter (usually a teen or grown adult), I always ask the same question: "What did your parents do right that resulted in your strong faith in Christ?"

Each time, without fail, I have heard the same answer:

"My parents were the same offstage and onstage. They were the same at home as they were in public. What you see is what you get. They are the real deal." Wow! That is what I want my kids and grand-kids to say about me. I want to be the real deal.

Recently, I was conversing with another mom who has raised children who also love and serve Jesus. As we chatted about how we raised our kids and what their day-to-day lives looked like, a set of verses in Deuteronomy came up as a common denominator:

> These commandments that I give you today are to be on
> your hearts. Impress them on your children. Talk about
> them when you sit at home and when you walk along the
> road, when you lie down and when you get up. Tie them as
> symbols on your hands and bind them on your foreheads.
> Write them on the doorframes of your houses and on your
> gate (Deuteronomy 6:6-9).

Weave the Truth into your life and into your family life. Talk about the Truth as you go about all of your daily routines, and make it a focal point sometime each day in your discussions. Have a simple family devotion time each day. Our general rule was that devotions would last one minute for each year of age of the youngest person. So if our youngest was age three, the devotions would be just three minutes long—and usually active!

You need the Truth, and everyone else in your world—your spouse, your family, your friends and coworkers, and even people you have yet to meet—need you to love the truth of God's Word. They also need you to love living it out. They want you to be real. Authentic. Genuine.

What memorial will you place in your home, in your room, on your desk, or on your mirror to remember that blessings come to those who live true?

CHAPTER 5

Becoming Relational

I unwrapped the gift the leadership team had given me for speaking. Three lovely boxes tied with golden ribbon. Out of the boxes came three angels. They were fun, folksy, and fantastic reminders to me of all that it takes to make relationships work. Their names were etched into ribbons they held: Faith, Hope, and Love.

Because Bill and I are the codirectors of a ministry called Love-Wise, we spend the majority of our time helping people give and receive love by connecting them to God's wisdom.

The Bible tells us what love looks like:

> Love is patient, love is kind and is not jealous; love does not brag and is not arrogant, does not act unbecomingly; it does not seek its own, is not provoked, does not take into account a wrong suffered, does not rejoice in unrighteousness, but rejoices with the truth; bears all things, believes all things, hopes all things, endures all things. Love never fails...And now these three remain: faith, hope and love. But the greatest of these is love (1 Corinthians 13:4-8,13).

Let's learn a little from those angels: Faith, Hope, and Love.

Angel of Faith

Women who love lavishly have an ability to see the potential, the positive, and the promise—not the problem. Check out this definition

Need To Remember

of faith from Hebrews 11:1 in the Amplified version of the Bible: "Now faith is the assurance (the confirmation, the title deed) of the things [we] hope for, being the proof of things [we] do not see and the conviction of their reality [faith perceiving as real fact what is not revealed to the senses]."

Faith is like a postdated check. We can't get our hands on the money yet, but we know one day we will. In the same way, a woman of faith sees the promise as just as good as the potential. Her faith helps her function in the realm of "what can be." She leans on God's power to see people from God's point of view, not just her own.

There are numerous times when I have needed to put on my rose-colored glasses through prayer to help me see the potential in a person. One of the verses I claim when I am looking at a negative situation, traits, or behaviors in a person is Romans 4:16-17: "Therefore, [inheriting] the promise is the outcome of faith and depends [entirely] on faith, Who gives life to the dead and speaks of the nonexistent things that [He has foretold and promised] as if they [already] existed" (AMP).

Faith gives us the ability to see things that are not as they are. So when I am concerned about my relationship with someone, or someone's character, choices, or behaviors, I will print out verses of what I believe God would want them to be or become—what God might want for his or her life (or my own)—and I pray these verses until I see the breakthrough. Sometimes I have prayed those verses for years in faith that God will move on behalf of that person, or me, or give a breakthrough that might reflect His character.

When one of our sons was struggling with his life and faith choices in college, I printed out all the verses that described how a godly man should look and act. I prayed those verses over him (and in some cases with him). About a year later, he called and said, "Mom, I picked up two copies of *The Purpose Driven Life*. Would you like to do this with me? We could read it at the same time and we could talk for a few minutes each day on the phone. Do you have time for that?" I made time for that! That breakthrough continues to bring fruit. This same son often calls and reads us quotes from books by some of his favorite authors and leaders. He e-mails and tweets inspiring verses and quotations to us to keep us encouraged. Now he is a part of our prayer and support team.

By praying for what you desire by faith, you keep your heart and mind on the positive! I encourage you to pray those verses out loud because three goals are accomplished:

- You hear the promises so your faith is built.
- Satan hears the promises and he must flee when the truth is spoken.
- God hears the promises and His heart moves to encourage you and work the situation for everyone's good and His glory.

Remember: It just takes a LITTLE faith to make a BIG difference! What person or situation in your world needs the eyes of faith to bring desired change?

> Truly I tell you, if you have faith as small as a mustard seed, you can say to this mountain, "Move from here to there," and it will move. Nothing will be impossible for you (Matthew 17:20).

Our words don't change things.
It's God's power applied to *His* words that change things!

● Angel of Hope

Hope can be hard to nail down. When I am trying to grasp an ethereal concept or wrap my mind around a difficult-to-understand truth, I often…

1. Read the entire context of the relevant Scripture passage.
2. Look at many translations or paraphrases of that same verse.

3. Read as many verses as possible on the subject in it to try to find God's definition of the word.

In the Old Testament, hope is often accompanied by the word *wait*. So hope is like a security deposit of God's love. We know that someday we will see the fullness of the answer, but for now, we just have a glimpse.

In the New Testament hope captures the idea of putting one's expectation in the person (God) who can do something about what you are hoping for! Hope is about your trusting in God, not your own ability.

Hope is placing a little more of your confidence in God day after day until you see the answer, or until you have total peace that the answer will come in God's timing.

Hope is the feeling you had as a kid on Christmas Eve, or the night before the last day of school. Hope is opening that fresh box of crayons and dreaming of what great art will be drawn. Hope is the new dress for the class picture, the prom, or the wedding day. Hope is excited about life. Hope is enthusiastic. Hope is energetic. Hope throws confetti before the parade begins. Hope sends out the party invitations months before (or sometimes years!) before the celebration will be held. Hope holds on and holds out for life's best. Hope looks for the creative way to keep a promise of love.

One of my favorite passages about hope is Romans 5:3-5:

> We also glory in our sufferings, because we know that suffering produces perseverance; perseverance, character; and character, hope. And hope does not put us to shame, because God's love has been poured out into our hearts through the Holy Spirit, who has been given to us.

No matter how bad things seem, God pours out love. Hope doesn't disappoint. Hope changes us! I believe this means God pulls back the curtains and lets us see the situation from a more heavenly viewpoint, and that is what keeps our heart hoping. Hope stokes the fires of love.

Angel of Love

Lavish love is infinite. It just keeps extending all that is good, kind, and true forever—not because a person deserves it but just because it is right to be loving.

There is no downside to becoming a loving person. Love makes us a better reflection of God. We will spend the remainder of the chapter looking at some of what love encompasses and how love can affect the relationships that matter most to you.

Three Simple Questions for Relationship Success

Our behaviors and choices really come down to our asking and answering three questions. These questions are contained in the sentences Jesus spoke in John 15:12-14: "My command is this: Love each other as I have loved you. Greater love has no one than this: to lay down one's life for one's friends. You are my friends if you do what I command."

Question 1: Do I really know how to love others? ("Love each other as I have loved you.")

Question 2: Do I believe God really loves me? ("Greater love has no one than this: to lay down one's life for one's friends.")

Question 3: Do I really love God? ("You are my friends if you do what I command.")

God's Kind of Love

The Bible is a love letter from God to you. It is the story of how God created you and made a plan to live by and a path to walk down. Even when we fall short in our imperfection, God loved us so much that He laid down His own life to pay the penalty for our sins. Because of His sacrifice, we can be spared the punishment of separation from God after death. And in this earthly life, Christ's death in our place redeemed us so we could live free from the grasp of unhealthy choices and addictions. We are free to love like God loves—without limits.

Life and love are possible through God's power, not just
our own!

So let's sum it up. God has a plan to give you a future, a hope, an abundant life here on earth, and then an eternity enjoying His love and presence forever. Now that is LOVE!

God's Love Is the Authentic Love

God is the Author of all love. God's very essence, His core being, is love. He invented love, and all other loves are either reproductions or counterfeits. Anything good, beautiful, and wonderful in this world is an expression of God's love for us. And things dark, twisted, harmful, confusing, toxic—those are Satan's distortions, his twisted forgery.

First John 4 has a lot to say about love. To help process this view of love from God's view, take a red pen and underline each mention of the word *love*. I have already underlined the phrase "God is love" for emphasis:

> Dear friends, let us love one another, for love comes from God. Everyone who loves has been born of God and knows God. Whoever does not love does not know God, because God is love. This is how God showed his love among us: He sent his one and only Son into the world that we might live through him. This is love: not that we loved God, but that he loved us and sent his Son as an atoning sacrifice for our sins. Dear friends, since God so loved us, we also ought to love one another. No one has ever seen God; but if we love one another, God lives in us and his love is made complete in us.

> This is how we know that we live in him and he in us: He has given us of his Spirit. And we have seen and testify that the Father has sent his Son to be the Savior of the world. If anyone acknowledges that Jesus is the Son of God, God lives in them and they in God. And so we know and rely on the love God has for us.

God is love. Whoever lives in love lives in God, and God in them. This is how love is made complete among us so that we will have confidence on the day of judgment: In this world we are like Jesus. There is no fear in love. But perfect love drives out fear, because fear has to do with punishment. The one who fears is not made perfect in love.

We love because he first loved us (1 John 4:7-19).

So what did you learn about God's incredible love? Let's pause and be overwhelmed by the love of God for a moment, shall we?

God's Love for You

In the Old Testament, God's love is most often referred to as "lovingkindness." This isn't an easy word to translate, but in the original Hebrew it also encompassed the ideas of mercy, steadfast love, and loyalty. It's a sure love that will never let go and will never be destroyed. It's a love that will be faithful even when we're not.

In God's lovingkindness, He's withheld the punishment that we deserve. His mercy is greater than our sin. Rejoice in the fact that God's love is an unfailing love based on His character rather than ours!

I am a Nana, and all of my grandchildren have their favorite blankets. They sleep with them, and after naptime, one of my favorite moments is when they toddle out of their room carrying their favorite blankets and crawl into my arms to rock with Nana for a little while until they are ready to face the rest of their day. God's love is like the precious way we feel when we are all wrapped up safely in the arms of someone who loves us! Once you are wrapped in the blanket of God's love, you never want to live life without it!

Broken to Beautiful

God has the ability to make the broken beautiful. It is much like the Japanese art of *kintsukuroi*, which is the repairing of pottery with gold or silver so that the piece is more beautiful and more valuable than before it was broken.

Two of my favorite women of the Bible are Naomi and Ruth. The book of Ruth opens with a scene where Naomi's husband, Elimelech, is walking in fear and not faith. He has taken his family to a foreign land, Moab, that doesn't know God. His two sons have married women from Moab, Orpah and Ruth. Now Elimelech and his two sons have died, leaving three widows in a land plagued by famine. Sounds like some pretty desperate straits, right?

Orpah goes back to her family of origin (which is what many people do in a crisis or time of stress—they hang on to the known dysfunction and refuse to step into the unknown plan, even if it might prove to be a much better, healthier choice). Naomi is so depressed that she renames herself "Mara," which means *bitter.* The women are at a fork in the road.

We each have a choice to love like God, in the same way Ruth has a choice. She could go home to her family, but instead she chooses to stay with her mother-in-law, not knowing what the consequences will be.

Naomi's wise choice was to love God enough to go back home to the people, the place, and the promise where she knew she would hear God and experience fellowship with God and God's people. Ruth's wise choice was to follow Naomi and follow the God of Naomi out of her love for both.

When you don't know what to do,
go back to the people, the places,
and the promises of God—
where you know you last heard God and
where you can hear from Him again.

Read the whole book of Ruth in one sitting and you will see a beautiful love story. It's a love story of God for his people, of a daughter and mother-in-law, and of two God-revering singles, Ruth and Boaz, who express their love for God by doing "the next right thing." And God provides to all three people a path of hope and provision.

Boy gets girl: Boaz marries a loving, godly, beautiful wife.

Girl gets boy: Ruth marries a wealthy man with strong standing in the community.

Grandma gets grandchild: Naomi gets a grandchild who is in the lineage of the Messiah!

They all get to see faith, hope, and love work as God braided them together into the "happily ever after" you and I have likely prayed for at some point in our own lives.

New View of Love

In the New Testament, we gain a greater explanation of why God loves each of us and what outcome God longs for in our lives as a result of His love.

There are three words that explain just how complete God's love is for us. Each declares the principle of why the God who created everything would leave the glory of heaven and come as a man, Jesus, to live among sinners. Jesus lived without sinning and eventually died in our place, paying the penalty for our sin.

These three words mean the difference between living eternally condemned and living eternally free.

Propitiation. This is a spiritual transaction of reconciliation. When the Jewish people were held in captivity by Egyptians as slaves, God raised up a leader, Moses, to confront the Pharaoh and secure the release of His people to return to their promised land. God sent ten plagues to get Pharaoh's attention. One of the plagues was the death of every firstborn Egyptian. God instructed all Jews to kill a spotless lamb and paint their doors with its blood so the Angel of Death would pass over their homes. (The Jewish holiday Passover celebrates how God saved His people that night and rescued them from both death and slavery.) From that time forward until Jesus came to earth and died, God required a sacrificial lamb as a symbolic atonement each year.

Jesus was born of a virgin and the Spirit, so Jesus was a lamb without blemish. First Peter 1:18-19 proclaims, "It was not with perishable things such as silver or gold that you were redeemed from the empty way of life handed down to you from your ancestors, but with the precious blood of Christ, a lamb without blemish or defect." And when John the Baptist was preparing the path for Christ, he declared, "Look, the Lamb of God, who takes away the sin of the world!" (John 1:29).

John was prophesying that Jesus was the sacrificial holy Lamb, the one who would atone for our sins.

Jesus the Lamb was our propitiation, paying the penalty for the sins of all people, for all time. This payment needed to be made because a Holy God and sin are not compatible. A sinless Lamb was required to appease the wrath of God. The Lamb of God reconciled our relationship with the Holy God. "Since we have now been justified by his blood, how much more shall we be saved from God's wrath through him!" (Romans 5:9).

Redemption. This is a commercial transaction that leads to freedom. A slave could be redeemed—that is, freed—from his master. Jesus bought us from the ultimate human trafficker, Satan, and the payment made was his very life in exchange for ours. If this were a movie, the crowd would be on its feet applauding the heroism of one sacrificing His life for another!

Christ gave His life for ours out of love, making us friends (John 15:13)—and He did this while we were still His enemies (Romans 5:8)!

> Surely he took up our pain and bore our suffering, yet we considered him punished by God, stricken by him, and afflicted. But he was pierced for our transgressions, he was crushed for our iniquities; the punishment that brought us peace was on him, and by his wounds we are healed. We all, like sheep, have gone astray, each of us has turned to our own way; and the Lord has laid on him the iniquity of us all (Isaiah 53:4-6).

When we didn't even know we could or should love God, God displayed and proved His love for us. He redeemed us by trading places with us, setting us free while He was beaten in our place.

Justification. This is a legal transaction of acquittal. The best picture of this term can be found in 2 Corinthians 5:21: "God made him who had no sin to be sin for us, so that in him we might become the righteousness of God."

Picture a courtroom. You are on trial for your life, and you are guilty. There must be a payment for breaking the law. The verdict comes in and you are convicted of that crime. But then the judge takes off his robes and steps in to take your death sentence. This judge, who has never done anything wrong, takes the lethal injection in your place, or in this case, on the cross. Your rap sheet with the long list of sins is exchanged for his blank one.

In today's terms, Christ was your substitute in the gas chamber. Christ put His head on your chopping block. Christ took the noose from your neck and placed it around His own. Why would Christ do all this? His love compelled him to look for a way to both fulfill the need of the law to have a payment, yet not require you to be that payment. He also made sure the payment would be for every human for all time and eternity. The only person who could die and make that atoning sacrifice would be a sinless one, and only one person fits that bill: Jesus, who was conceived by the Holy Spirit. Only Jesus could be the one to take your place and mine, and He volunteered to die for us. Today, in our vocabulary, we have a term for this: He is our hero!

Our hero, Christ, did all this so we could live righteous and free. First Peter 2:24 says, "'He himself bore our sins' in his body on the cross, so that we might die to sins and live for righteousness; 'by his wounds you have been healed.'"

Max Lucado sums up this deep steadfast love and its relationship to our imperfect humanity: "God loves you just the way you are, but He refuses to leave you that way. He wants you to be just like Jesus."

When I feel torn between my will and God's will, I picture Jesus, stretched out on the cross in my place because He loved me and gave the ultimate sacrifice. At that moment, I am compelled to express my love by choosing to follow His plan and path for me. I would never want to knowingly and purposefully grieve the heart of the One who went to hell and back to rescue and redeem me.

The path of love for Jesus was to the cross,
where He stretched out His arms to die for me.
The path of love for me is to the cross to kneel
in obedience to Him.

Love Doesn't Trip Up Others

Because love is an esteemed value, our goal should be to not be a stumbling block that causes others to sin.

When the church was being founded, some believers would buy meat that had been sacrificed to idols. They didn't see anything wrong with it because it was decent meat and they didn't believe in any powers having to do with idols. However, other new converts from idol worship still attached all the pagan behaviors and curses to the meat itself. The apostle Paul gave those believers some sound advice that resonates for us as well:

> Be careful, however, that the exercise of your rights does not become a stumbling block to the weak. For if someone with a weak conscience sees you, with all your knowledge, eating in an idol's temple, won't that person be emboldened to eat what is sacrificed to idols? So this weak brother or sister, for whom Christ died, is destroyed by your knowledge. When you sin against them in this way and wound their weak conscience, you sin against Christ. Therefore, if what I eat causes my brother or sister to fall into sin, I will never eat meat again, so that I will not cause them to fall (1 Corinthians 8:9-13).

Today we could insert any number of gray areas: drinking, gambling, the clothes we wear, the cars we drive, the media we watch, and so on. We have great freedom, but how will we use that freedom? For ourselves, indulging our rights? Or shall we lay down certain rights for the greater responsibility of being a conduit of love to the weak so they can be linked to the strong love of God?

Love is volunteering to carry another's pack until they are strong enough to carry it themselves.

Love Like God!

Let's take a closer look at how 1 Corinthians 13, the "Love Chapter," can play out in our lives on a daily basis. Love is...

- Patient. It is willing to wait.
- Kind. It is gentle in behavior.
- Does not envy. It doesn't let jealousy boil up in relationships.
- Does not brag about its own accomplishments.
- Not rude or indecent.
- Not self-seeking. It doesn't go after its own interests.
- Not easily angered. It does not become irritated quickly and it avoids sharpness of spirit.
- Keeps no record of wrongs. It does not record the bad things others have done.
- Does not delight in evil. It finds no joy when wickedness triumphs.
- Rejoices with the truth. It finds delight in everything true.
- Protects. It covers like a roof.
- Trusts. It puts faith in people without being gullible.
- Hopes. It looks on the bright side and does not despair.
- Perseveres. It carries on like a stout-hearted soldier.
- Never fails. It survives everything.

What trait of being loving is the most challenging for you right now? Fortify that area with these tips:

- *Investigate:* Look up all the Bible verses with that word in it. Get a good handle on what God meant by the use of that term.

- *Intercede:* Pray God gives you opportunities to practice that trait of love.

- *Instruct:* Teach others (your children, a class, or simply be a role model at work or in your personal life). The more you exercise that trait, the stronger and more skilled you will become at that trait of love.

Love Reaches Out of Its Comfort Zone

First Peter 1:22 tells us to "love one another deeply, from the heart." How can we love deeply? And why would we want to? How can we love fervently, enthusiastically, eagerly, energetically, intently?

This can be a challenge because people can be hard to love. (You can be hard to love and I know I can be hard to love!) We all have our issues, and these quirks get on others' nerves. People, even people we love, can really tick us off! And some require more patient, fervent love than others! One of my friends calls the hard-to-love folks "EGRs." *Extra Grace Required.*

The thing you love about someone can drive you crazy too. It is like two sides of a coin, and you need a way to turn the coin over and remember, "Oh yeah! That's why I love them! That is the quality I admire."

My husband, Bill, loves his coffee. But along with Bill's love of coffee, he also has an annoying habit: He'll often forget to place his dirty mugs in the sink or dishwasher. I find dirty coffee cups every place imaginable: in the garage, in the car, in the truck, in the closet, on the sidewalk, on the deck and patio, in the shop, in the office, on the stairwell, in the bathroom—you name it, and I have likely found a coffee cup there.

I am not a coffee drinker really. I might sip a nonfat latte from time to time, but for the most part, coffee makes my heart race, and I prefer that only Bill makes my heart skip a beat! Bill says that I am naturally caffeinated by God, and it takes Bill drinking three cups of coffee just to keep up with my energy. Coffee is a part of what makes Bill…well, Bill! But this dirty coffee mug habit became a silent resentment I carried. I was letting myself be offended by his choice to not get mugs to the sink.

One day, as we were preparing to move homes, I was doing that last load of dishes and I realized it was entirely composed of coffee mugs! I prayed something like, "Lord, change him!" But instead God wisely chose to change me!

The Spirit of God will often whisper verses to get your attention. "Pam, remember that verse about loving deeply? This would be a good time to use that principle. And Pam, remember that love covers over a multitude of sins. Bill is a good man, and your love could cover this habit by extending mercy. I asked you to bless those who persecute you. You are feeling a bit persecuted, aren't you? Well, blessing is the path to love."

I decided to pray a blessing over Bill every time I saw one of his empty displaced mugs. I would pray things like, "Let Bill be the head and not the tail," "Let everything Bill puts his hands to prosper," and "Let Bill be known in the gates."

I started to smile when I saw dirty coffee mugs, and thought, "This blessing thing is working! I am hardly upset at all anymore!" So then I started praying blessings when I saw Bill with a clean or full mug, and that made me love him more, so I thought, "I choose to bless Bill when I see any coffee mug, anywhere at any time!" We travel about 250 days a year, and many of those days are in airports. Nearly everyone in an airport has a coffee mug, so my man gets blessed all day long every day!

As I have embraced the ever-reappearing dirty coffee mug by responding with a prayer of blessing, my anger and annoyance have been replaced with fond affection. Now if I locate a dirty mug in some unusual place, it is a symbol of God's ability to help me love as He loves. Each mug is also a reminder to me of my hardworkin' man who requires a little caffeine to do all the wonderful acts of service that benefit so many—including me.

God's transformation has helped me overcome so much that I look for new ways to put a smile on Bill's face with coffee. For Bill's fiftieth birthday we celebrated with a family trip to visit a coffee farm. He selected the beans, roasted them to perfection, and designed the label for his own "Bill Farrel blend." What was my gift to him on that fiftieth birthday? A coffee mug, of course!

While this is a lighthearted example of how to show love outside your comfort zone, I have been a part of the prayer teams of women who have fervently loved...

- Children off drugs or drinking and away from foolish friends.
- Husbands out of addictions or unproductive habits.
- Family members away from shackling temptations.
- Friends out of Satan's grip to God's grace.
- Coworkers and volunteer team members from negative attitudes to positive performance.
- Mentees and disciples toward holiness and away from destructive life patterns.

I have a friend, Dr. Gail Hayes, who works in the inner city with at-risk youth. One day she was sharing a story of a mother in the projects who came to her crying. She had all but given up her son to the streets and gangs. The mother wailed, "I am so afraid for my son. The Devil has my boy in his death grip. I am afraid he is going straight to Hell."

To which Dr. Hayes replied, "Then you go love the Hell right out of that boy!"

Toxic Love

If a characteristic of a healthy relationship is loving as God loves, then a toxic relationship would be characterized by the opposite of that love. Let's rewrite the familiar 1 Corinthians 13 passage on love as if Satan had turned it inside out and backward.

A toxic relationship is impatient and unkind. It is always

envious and jealous. It boasts and is self-glorifying. It is arrogant and proud, self-centered and rude. It easily loses its temper and keeps track of all offenses and holds a grudge. It is thrilled when people look and feel stupid. It loves a mistake because the error can be replayed over and over. It runs to evil, never protects others, and gives up on people and life easily.

Toxic relationships poison the Golden Rule and turn it into, *Do unto others before they do it to you. Exploit others before they exploit you.* And they would scoff at Jesus's example of sacrificing for others. Instead, they would sacrifice others for their own benefit or entertainment.

A toxic relationship is just what it sounds like: a place to dump poison, hazardous waste, dangerous toxins, and life-killing sewage. Jesus comes to give life abundantly; the thief (Satan) comes to kill, steal, and destroy (John 10:10). If someone is killing your hopes, dreams, and self-esteem, if they are stealing your future, your safety, or your money, if they are destroying your reputation, your peace of mind, or your property—chances are they are toxic!

If you leave someone's presence and you feel closer to God, you've made a healthy decision. If you feel like Satan has just worked you over, you've encountered a toxic person. One can minister to a toxic person, but you are on dangerous ground if you date or marry one. It will even be hard to be close friends with someone if they are toxic and unwilling to get help.

Leslie Vernick, author of *The Emotionally Destructive Relationship*, gives this test to help you know if a person in your life is safe or toxic:

1. One or both parties commit physical, emotional, verbal, or sexual abuse upon the other.

2. One person is regularly overprotective, overbearing, or both toward the other.

3. One person is over dependent upon the other to affirm his or her personal value and worth, to meet all of his or her needs, and to make most of his or her decisions.

4. One person demonstrates a pattern of deceiving the other through lying, hiding, pretending, misleading, or twisting information to make something appear other than what it is.

5. One person exhibits chronic indifference or neglect toward thoughts, feelings, or well-being of the other.[1]

Leslie is a licensed clinical social worker, so helping people deal with toxic relationships has become an area of expertise. In a nutshell, Leslie shares how you can deal with your toxic person in an easy-to-remember three-step process. (The process is Leslie's, but I have summarized it in my own words.)

Speak up. Voice your hurt, pain, or discomfort to the person who is hurting you. When you express your hurt, pain, or frustration to a healthy person, that person will want to fix the relationship and find some kind of win-win. A toxic person will dismiss your pain. Develop a plan for how you will respond if a toxic person continues to hurt you. If they continue, then you will…

Stand up. If the person continues their destructive behaviors, explain to them the consequences. If they still continue to hurt you, then you will…

Step back. Pull away from the relationship far enough to feel safe. Follow through on the natural consequences you explained previously. Set boundaries in place to protect the remnant of the relationship and give God time to work to heal that person—and to heal your heart and hurts.

Heart-Healthy Connections

Bill and I have years of personal experience learning how to lay out healthy boundaries. Bill has a family member who struggles with mental illness and she often rages, acts on illogical thoughts, and is then cruel, unkind, or unthinking of others' needs around her. And as you have heard me mention, my father had a pain in his heart that he soothed with alcohol instead of a relationship with God.

Each of us in our family had to come to a place where we asked God how to love Dad, yet set a boundary with him so he would have someone left to love him when God did eventually reach him.

Boundaries protect a relationship from the toxic person. Boundaries give God time to reach the broken and dysfunctional soul. Boundaries safely shelter the relationship so once the person does respond to God's healing touch, they have a relationship to return to— they haven't destroyed it. Boundaries show love by protecting the toxic person from themselves and their own destructive choices.

I had to set a series of boundaries, one after another. First, I decided not to ride in my dad's car if I suspected he had been drinking. I would meet Dad someplace or I would offer to drive. He didn't like it at first, but soon he adjusted to my new way of relating to him.

Then I laid a boundary that when I came to stay with him, if he drank or raised his voice or his hand, I would simply stand up and drive away. I never went to my dad's place alone to stay the night. When I married and had children, Dad was never left alone with my kids, and they never rode in his car if he had been drinking (which I assumed was most of the time). The majority of the time, Bill and I invited Dad to join us at our home, in our car, in our life, on our turf, and he learned to live by our healthier guidelines for life.

I didn't set any of those boundaries to hurt my dad. Rather, I laid each boundary out of love and concern for him. I laid boundaries hoping to save Dad's life and the lives of others. I wanted to see the day God would save his soul and save him from his self-destructive patterns.

We cannot control others' choices,
but we can control our responses to others' choices.

Forgiveness Sets Your Heart Free

Many of us are carrying a backpack of bitterness around and it is keeping us from getting and keeping life together. Our pain is keeping us shackled from our potential and promise.

Bill and I looked at the great work God had done to break us free from our past, free from the dysfunction and free from the pain and baggage of our youth. When we studied how God had set us free to break the negative patterns, it all led back to the cross. The cross is where unconditional love, forgiveness, mercy, and grace meet. The cross is the key to a healthy future.

Embracing God's view of love allows us to love.

But to truly live and love freely, we must turn the key of forgiveness on the jail cell of our hurt. Bill looked at all Christ had accomplished on the cross and asked, "What if we took what Jesus did on the cross and applied those principles to an interpersonal relationship? What would forgiveness look like?"

God led Bill to pen the *Six Steps of Forgiveness*. Colossians 3:13 raises the bar when it says, "Bear with each other and forgive one another if any of you has a grievance against someone. Forgive as the Lord forgave you." In other words, we are called to forgive everybody for everything. The best way I know of to keep short accounts is to follow this simple process. Read these statements out loud.

1. I forgive [name] for [offense] (1 John 1:9).

   Talk about what's gone wrong and ask God to bring specific healing to your heart.

2. I admit that what happened was wrong (Romans 3:23).

   We live in a world that doesn't like to say anything is wrong because that isn't politically correct. But if nothing has been done wrong, there is nothing to forgive. It could just be an attitude of yours that needs to be adjusted. God will show you if this is your attitude or their offense that will need to be forgiven.

3. I do not expect this person to make up for what he or she has done (2 Corinthians 5:17).

   A lot of time we live our lives on hold, waiting for the person to make up for what he or she has done, but chances are the person that wounded you might never come ask for forgiveness. Don't delay your healthy living, waiting for the toxic person to ask for forgiveness.

4. I will not use the offense to define who this person is (Ephesians 2:12-13).

   Do not label someone by their offense. If you call the person the victimizer, that makes you the victim, and you do not want to live with a victim mentality. You want to choose to see yourself and all people as God sees us—in need of a Savior, a Redeemer, and a Restorer.

5. I will not manipulate this person with this offense (Psalm 130:4).

   Give up your right to pick up the past and use it to beat someone up or push their emotional buttons. People sometimes ask, "I am just supposed to let that person off the hook?" No. Just take them off your hook and place them on God's hook, and let God deal out consequences.

6. I will not allow what has happened to stop my personal growth (2 Peter 3:18).

   This might be the most vital step. Commit to doing whatever it takes, whatever God asks, to get healthy and well. Get in the Word for yourself and dig out the verses that God can use to help you overcome.

If you can't sincerely get through all six statements, ask God to prepare your heart to be able to forgive. (Sometimes I pray, "God, give me the desire to forgive.") God has the wisdom to know exactly how to lead you to a place of complete freedom from bitterness.

Bless to Live Blessed

God gives us some specific commands to bless and be a blessing so we can live free.

> Bless those who curse you, pray for those who mistreat you (Luke 6:28).

> Bless those who persecute you; bless and do not curse…Live in harmony with one another…If it is possible, as far as it depends on you, live at peace with everyone. Do not take revenge, my dear friends, but leave room for God's wrath, for it is written: "It is mine to avenge; I will repay," says the Lord. On the contrary: "If your enemy is hungry, feed him; if he is thirsty, give him something to drink. In doing this, you will heap burning coals on his head." Do not be overcome by evil, but overcome evil with good (Romans 12:14,16,18-21).

When I read these verses in a quiet time with God as a young mom, I knew even though I had already forgiven my dad for every hurt and pain I could remember, God was calling me to be a blessing. I knew God wanted me to write a story that would share the love of God with my dad and open the door of grace and mercy for him.

So I prayed, "God, I am having a hard time finding a happy memory. If You help me remember one, I will write a blessing and give it to Dad for Christmas." That night as I dreamt, I remembered a precious day when I was a very young girl. I got up early and wrote the blessing. I had it framed and prepared my heart. I knew I had to give the blessing expecting nothing in return, and I should even be prepared for a negative response.

On Christmas Day, I called Dad aside so it was just him and me. I read this blessing to my father.

It was a sunny Saturday morning. Excited children piled out of cars, baskets in hand. It was the day before Easter, the day of our small town's big egg hunt. I was nervous and excited, as were all the other preschoolers. I held tight to my dad's hand. The whistle blew, and the race to find the prized golden egg was on! I picked up a pink egg and then a green one, and I placed them gently in my basket. But what I really wanted was that golden egg. The hunt seemed as though it lasted a lifetime. It seemed that no one could find the golden egg. .

Dad said, "Come here, honey."

He bent down and whispered into my ear and pointed at the ground. I looked down at a disgusting sight—an egg smashed and broken from being trampled upon by tiny feet.

"But it's broken!" I said to my dad.

"What color is it, honey?"

I shrugged my shoulders.

"Look close. What color do you see?"

I tried hard to find a piece of shell big enough to discern its color. I picked up a small fragment and whispered, "It's gold! Daddy, it's gold!" But how was I supposed to get it over to the judges?

"Pick it up. Moms and dads can't touch the prized egg. You have to carry it."

"Ick! It's too yucky, Daddy! I can't."

"If you want the prize, you have to pick it up. But I will help you carry it."

We bent down and I scooped up as much of the egg remnant as my tiny hands could carry. It felt awful. Dad slid his hand under mine, and together we carried our broken treasure to the judges. I was awarded a huge basket brimming with Easter goodies. Dad was proud of me, and I was proud of him.

My dad is a lot like that broken golden egg. He has often felt inadequate to be all that he wanted to be as a dad. His heart is like that egg—full of prizewinning potential but cracked by the heartache of broken dreams. Dad has a heart of gold, but it often goes unseen by those around him. Words fail him. Sometimes his actions fall short of the feelings he'd like to express. But I've always held on to a piece of that prizewinning potential, just like I held on to that small piece of golden shell. I've held on to the golden moments that Dad and I have shared. Like that day in the park, when I was proud of him and he was proud of me. And when times are hard, I sometimes hear that whisper, "If you want the prize, you have to pick it up." So I gather up the pieces of life and carry what life requires me to carry.

No, Dad is not perfect, but neither am I. So I hold tight to that less-than-perfect treasure because all that has happened—the good and the bad—God has used to make me the woman I've wanted to be. I have become a woman who can look at a bad situation, find the gold in it, and go on.

I'm a prizewinner in my daddy's eyes, and his love is a golden treasure to me.

As I handed him the framed blessing, he began to weep. A man who had never read any of my writing (that I knew of), a man who had never heard any of my speeches, complimented me, and he blessed me back: "Thank you for using your fine words to say such nice things about this good ol' bad ol' boy. If you think sharing our story might help other folks, you just share it then." And he gave me a rare hug and wiped away his tears.

Not many weeks later, I couldn't get Dad on the phone. I called the sheriff's department and asked them to do a drive-by to check on him. About midnight, I got the call that my father had passed from this life.

I was the executor of the will and had his house key, so immediately, I met my siblings at his home. When I walked in, though his body had been taken by the coroner, I could tell where he had spent his last hours. There at his desk was the stack of Christian books and videos each of the family members had given him. The resources had been read, dog-eared, and watched. Sitting on top of the pile was a *Steps to Peace with God* booklet. (We later learned a neighbor had given it to him a day or two before he died.) The booklet was opened to the prayer of surrender. Pulled forward, as if he had been reading it moments before he entered eternity, was the tribute I had written him.

I read the tribute one last time as I placed his ashes in the cold Kansas ground that winter. There was a sense of peace and freedom because I knew I had done everything I could to show Dad the love of God, and I believe he finally gave in to that persistent love. Our gracious God ushered him to heaven to finally live in peace.

The strength of your love can
become the strength of others' lives.

CHAPTER 6

Becoming Healthy

We women are so busy taking care of others we have a hard time taking care of ourselves. We've got a blind spot when it comes to our own needs—just like Jenny.

Jenny was driving erratically so the highway patrol pulled her over. Thinking she'd been driving drunk, they were about to give her a breath test when an accident happened on the other side of the road. They said to Jenny, "Stay here." But Jenny thought, *This is my chance to escape.* So she got in the car, drove home, and parked the car in the garage.

A few hours later there was a knock on the door. It was the highway patrol.

"Are you Jenny Smith?" the officer asked.

"Why, yes, I am."

"Were you pulled over and cited today for a traffic violation?"

"No sir, I have been home all day."

"Well, someone with your name and address was pulled over today. Perhaps if we just saw the car we could clear things up."

So Jenny led them out to the garage, thinking, *I am totally going to get away with this. It has been hours—the engine is nice and cold.* Then Jenny threw open the garage door...and there was the highway patrol car with its lights still flashing!

Jenny Smith had a blind spot. We all do. The lights are flashing in our garage too!

For many women, taking care of themselves is a blind spot. The Bible poses a question with clear intent: "Don't you know that you yourselves are God's temple and that God's Spirit dwells in your midst?" (1 Corinthians 3:16).

Take care of your temple. You are valuable! In the Sermon on the Mount, Jesus told His followers to "Look at the birds of the air; they do not sow or reap or store away in barns, and yet your heavenly Father feeds them. Are you not much more valuable than they?" (Matthew 6:26). You are more valuable than the birds and as valuable as my neighbor, because God's Spirit resides in you.

If you listen to the Spirit of God, the Spirit will help you
care for your "temple" – YOU!

I was a competitive gymnast, dancer, and cheerleader growing up, and then a competitive diver in college. Our family has always been physically active. Eight years ago, because of a health issue that hit my husband, our family had made even more significant changes to take better care of ourselves. But with a crazy travel schedule I was cutting some corners—not getting enough sleep, having a little sugar here and there, and too much sitting on airplanes and not enough walking in the park.

One day, God got my attention. Bill and I were preparing to speak at a high-altitude location. I got dizzy and my heart began to race, and then beat out of rhythm. I sent Bill ahead to do tech checks and I lay down, closed my eyes, and prayed. God's peace calmed and comforted me, but it took more than an hour to get my heart back in rhythm. That was a flashing yellow light to proceed with caution.

I had some blood tests done after that at a wellness week sponsored by First Place 4 Health, and the nurse called with bad news. The negative report shook me to the core. After all, I had been working out daily and eating well. But my weight kept going up, and now I was slapped in the face with a new reality. My health was at risk unless something dramatic changed! But I didn't know what to change.

Honestly, I took the news hard. My husband prayed with me and encouraged me to do whatever it took to get well. My friends provided cheerleading and sweet prayers. My personal trainer said, "You work out hard. You never miss a session. There is a thinner, healthier Pam inside—she is just bubble-wrapped!"

I went to bed and prayed, "Lord, You know how depressed I am. I have been encouraging women to live healthier but something is going very wrong in my body. I am such a failure. So I need some help here. Your Word says, *In peace I will lie down and sleep, for you alone, LORD, make me dwell in safety.* I need some safety in my thinking and in my body, so minister to me as I sleep. When I wake up tomorrow morning, please provide an answer so I might go forward and live long and strong for you."

I was physically and emotionally exhausted, and God was faithful to send slumber. But at five o'clock the next morning my phone vibrated and I picked it up to read this text message:

> Get up! God has set His alarm clock, and it is time to overcome every weight, every infirmity, every sickness, every bondage that has tried to strangle the physical, emotional, and spiritual life out of you. It doesn't matter how long you have been bound. Stop hitting the snooze button and GET UP! —Rod Parsley, World Harvest

I got up! I was ready to make the changes I needed!

I thought, "The definition of insanity is doing the same thing over and over and expecting a different result. Something needs to change. What is it, God?" If something wasn't working, I wanted to know exactly what that something was. As I reviewed my food journals and my activity log (I have worn a pedometer for years), I could see I was in the ballpark of what was healthy in my eating and activity. While I had skipped on some hours of sleep for a few stretches in the fall, for the most part, I was sleeping around seven hours on average. I am not a big caffeine consumer, so that couldn't be the problem. I felt I really didn't have adequate information on what was going wrong in my body.

My general physician was a traditional doctor, and her practice was so full that I usually only got a few minutes once a year with her. She simply did a few basic exams, asked the same questions, wrote out the same prescriptions, and gave the same warnings about working out and eating right. I had already met with several nutritionists through my insurance provider, but I thought I needed to get a second opinion. I needed to see a different doctor.

Bill and I have a ministry friend who is a respected doctor. However, his more holistic approach wasn't covered by our insurance. I hadn't seen him for many years because it was all out-of-pocket expense. But I thought, *If I am dead, I won't be able to earn money. Trying to save money on my medical treatment is what needs to change. I need to value my marriage, my family, my ministry, and my future enough to invest in me.*

I conversed with Dr. Stengler, sharing my test results. I made an appointment that was three weeks away, and in the meantime he advised me to be very strategic in my diet: lots of green vegetables, very little fruit, only lean meat and fish, no sugar, and no breads or grains. He also asked me to keep up my 10,000 steps a day. I did this, and by the time I saw him three weeks later, I had already lost 18 pounds.

He spent over an hour asking about my life, my habits, my routines, and my stress, and he ordered a more thorough panel of tests. I returned to hear the findings and he spent another hour explaining those test results and detailing out a course of action to get my health back on track.

The biggest problem was my current medication. When I told him I had been on a certain antibiotic for acne on and off since I was 16 (for over 35 years), his eyes widened in shock. He confirmed that the decades of antibiotic use was likely a significant reason my body had lost its ability to process food correctly. The antibiotics had killed the probiotics (good bacteria). I listened intently, and then I whined, "But I have to be on TV and speak, so what am I going to do about my acne?"

He assured me my diet change would help and topical external options were available. Then he gave me a dose of reality when he asked, "Are you ready to make the changes needed to save your life?"

"Yes," I said. "I guess my thinking has gotten kind of off-track. Let me run out this scenario: I keep taking antibiotics, I keep gaining weight and get full-blown diabetes, and I die. People come to my funeral, look in the casket, and say, *What a shame, she died so young.*

But look at her beautiful clear skin." I definitely had some priorities to straighten out!

We laid out a new Mediterranean-Paleo diet with lots of vegetables, a few fruits, and some lean protein. (Wheat and processed grains were part of my problem.) I rewarded every ten pounds lost with a new healthy kitchen tool or new workout outfit so I would continue to make wise nutrition choices. I met with a personal trainer and doubled my physical activity.

I knew I wanted to live long and strong for God. I also knew one of my books was going to be re-released under the new title *10 Secrets to Living Smart, Savvy, and Strong*—and I felt like none of that was true of me at that moment. Bill and I also powwowed and we selected the same word for our year: *Strong.*

We decided every choice and decision would be run through the grid of, "Will this make me stronger? Our marriage stronger? Our health stronger? Our business stronger? Our ministry stronger? Our family stronger?" We also selected a theme verse for the year: "Be strong and courageous. Do not be afraid; do not be discouraged, for the LORD your God will be with you wherever you go" (Joshua 1:9).

This was a perfect verse because it had the goal (be strong and courageous), but it also dealt with my emotions (don't be afraid; don't be discouraged). And because I travel so much, I loved the reminder that God will be with me wherever I go.

You don't become strong overnight. It's a process! And while we're in the process, God doesn't want us to get discouraged. He's saying, "Don't tremble, don't be dismayed. Don't let this shatter you!"

So I hung my heart on *strong*. I got a T-shirt with the word emblazoned on the front. I also printed out all the verses about being strong and staying strong, and that is where I spent my devotional time. Bill and I took a photo of us and a set of weights laid out to spell *strong*, and we made a poster of it with our verse and posted it in our offices. I downloaded songs that had *strong* in the title or lyrics. I tried to spend time with people who were strong physically, emotionally, spiritually, and financially in order to learn from them. And God made me strong enough to...

- call a new doctor, nutritionist, and trainer—and work the plan they laid out.

- believe He would cover the price of tests and other items I needed to stay strong.

- apply the wisdom the doctor gave me.

- be honest with friends and family so they could pray and support me.

- add more strength training to my exercise regimen.

- trust that if I slept I could still get done the work God needed me to do.

- reward myself with healthy things like fun workouts, kitchen equipment, new exercise wear, or an occasional spa day.

So what were the results of my *strong* year? I got strong! I shed over 50 pounds; I went from walking to running; I could lift more weights and my backaches disappeared. I moved from health risk to health strength. People began to use words like *svelte, power, fit,* and *radiant* when they spoke about my appearance. But this kind of strong goes to the core. I believe God can accomplish what seems impossible—in every area of life.

However, this is not a one-time journey for me. It is an every-day-for-the-rest-of-my-life battle that I must win. So each day I begin with a prayer: "Lord, give me strength!"

In what area of life do you need God to make you strong? Find a word that reflects this desire and make it your one-word prayer for the year. In *My One Word,* Pastor Mike Ashcroft shares an illustration for how this one word can work in your life. He hurt his foot and had to wear a boot. This boot held the bones in place so they could heal. He compared that process to the benefit of having a word for the year. "My foot needed to be held on the outside for the sake of what was going on on the inside. This is true of our spiritual lives. We need a boot, so to speak. Something to hold us in a given position long enough for some specific inner work to happen. My One Word can be that tool."[1]

Find a word that will move your life forward. Then select a verse that reflects the heart of this word, and dig in to learn as much about it as you can. So what is the word you need to hang your heart on this year?

My word is:

My verse is:

My motto is:

My song is:

My symbol is:

Then take a photo, buy an item of clothing, or a piece of art that reminds you of your word.

Live Long and Prosper

I pray this verse for everyone who reads my books or listens to me on media or sits in my audiences: "Dear friend, I pray that you may enjoy good health and that all may go well with you, even as your soul is getting along well" (3 John 2). I pray that you *prosper* in every area of your life.

In *10 Secrets to Living Smart, Savvy, and Strong*, I shared the results of several studies that examined people who lived to be 100. Below are a few characteristics they have in common. Read the list and choose a few things to apply to your life so you too can live longer and stronger for God.

- Be positive! Centenarians are cheerfulness and optimistic.
- Eat right! Lose weight. Centenarians are not obese.
- Quit! Centenarians rarely smoke.
- Chill! Centenarians have a stress-reduction mindset.
- Laugh! Centenarians have a sense of humor.
- Believe! Centenarians have a sense of hope.
- Enjoy! Centenarians have interests and hobbies.
- Volunteer! Centenarians care about others.
- Forgive! Centenarians release grudges.

- Adapt! Centenarians have the ability to cope with loss and change.
- Move! Centenarians are active.
- Love! Centenarians are in relationships.
- Think! Centenarians keep their minds active.
- Work! Centenarians are conscientious.

The one or two items off this list that I will work on this year are:

1.

2.

God will empower you to cross the finish line as a victor too!

Your Spiritual Life

While taking care of yourself so you can live longer and stronger for God is vital, it is too easy to move past taking good care of ourselves so we can serve God to worshipping ourselves and expecting God to serve us. What unravels a life is when you love yourself and your ways more than God's ways.

The world will tell you, "Look out for number one!" But God says, "You shall have no other gods before me" (Exodus 20:3).

Most of us do not achieve God's best.
We are wrapped up in ourselves instead of being
wrapped up in God's love for us.

Too many of us have crowned ourselves god of our world. The

problem with being too preoccupied with ourselves, however, is that we have little time to be occupied with God. If we try to be god of our world, it can only be as big as our own talent, skill, time, and energy. If we allow ourselves to follow God and God's will, then *all of who God is* becomes available to accomplishing God's plan and path for us.

It's all about motive: Why are you doing what you're doing? Who is getting the glory?

Why Do You Have to Be So Mean?

It can be hard to recognize our own selfishness. One way to identify these narcissistic tendencies is to take note of the moments when you get angry. Anger will be either righteous or unrighteous.

Jesus exhibited righteous anger when He turned over the tables in the temple. He saw everyone losing reverence and respect for the God who had created them. Christ was particularly upset with leaders who were using the poor and broken to gain worldly goods, looking out for their selfish needs instead of looking out for the well-being of the people. Righteous anger comes when we see God being blasphemed, mocked, or belittled, or when we see the people God loves being abused and mistreated.

Righteous anger protects God's glory and the people God loves. Unrighteous anger protects only our interests.

Unrighteous anger comes when we are upset that *our* table has been turned over; when we feel people around us are not giving *us* reverence and respect; when someone is standing in *our* way of gaining worldly goods; when we feel *our* glory is not being protected. As Proverbs 29:11 reminds us, "Fools give full vent to their rage, but the wise bring calm in the end."

Pride Goes Before the Fall

Pride and anger are usually all wrapped up together. This was Lucifer's downfall. He was created as a beautiful angel. Satan's original role was to lead out in worshipping God, but he decided he didn't like that plan and he wanted everyone to worship him. For his pride, God brought him low.

This self-worship usually isn't so overt in us. It usually just starts with a little selfish seed. Perhaps you have had one of these thoughts pass through your mind:

It's okay to party. I've earned it.

It's not an addiction. I have it under control.

I deserve this more than she does.

I'm not looking good here. I need a little white lie.

God calls that sin, but I can handle it.

That only happens to other people. I can beat the odds.

I don't want to think about the outcome. I just want to relax and get away from all this stress!

Let other people deal with it. I am out of here.

All sin starts as a seed, as simply the thought of sin. It is not a sin to first think it—we are all human. However, it is a sin to keep thinking it!

The danger zone is when we pause to ponder the sin. When we think, "I wonder how I could enjoy this sin, but not have it negatively impact me?" That should set off all kinds of alarms in our heart and mind. When we ponder sin and hold on to pride, the Spirit pulls the fire alarm of our lives to try to rescue us from ourselves.

A wise woman will learn to listen to the whisper of God's Spirit so she won't have to endure the shout of discipline.

Know Yourself

If we are going to love others as we love ourselves, it might be wise to know ourselves and know others more fully. Then we can relate to others in a healthy way. We all need a few tools in our relationship toolbox.

We can be irritated by the idiosyncrasies of others or we can value the differences and use the differences for us and for all our relationships.

Differences in Gender

God made men and women different before sin entered the world. And He did it on purpose! Genesis 1:27 tells us, "So God created mankind in his own image, in the image of God he created them; male and female he created them."

We believe He might have decided to create men and women because His character is too immense to be reflected in just one gender. To give us a more complete glimpse of the majestic Creator, He made man and woman, and then the two come together and are "one flesh." The New Testament says this is a mystery, a picture of Christ and the church, made for unity.

If we were made for unity, why do men and women get so frustrated with one another? If one can gain greater knowledge of the opposite gender and learn to value and appreciate them as a unique creation by God, we can learn to use those differences to everyone's benefit.

In the book *Men Are Like Waffles—Women Are Like Spaghetti*, we explain that men process life in boxes. Their thinking is divided up into boxes that have room for one issue and one issue only. The typical man spends time in one box at a time and one box only. When a man is at work, he is at work. When he is in the garage tinkering around, he is in the garage tinkering. When he is watching TV, he is watching TV! Social scientists call this "compartmentalizing."

As a result of thinking through life in boxes, men are by nature problem solvers. They enter a box, size up the "problem" that exists, and formulate a solution. A man will strategically organize his life in boxes and then spend most of his time in the boxes he can succeed in.

In contrast to men's approach, women are typically better at multitasking than men. A woman can talk on the phone, prepare a meal, make a shopping list, work on the planning for tomorrow's business meeting, give instructions to her children as they are going out to play, and close the door with her foot without skipping a beat!

Most women go through life by trying to make connections, so they solve problems by talking things through. This creates significant stress for couples because while she is making all the connections, he is frantically jumping boxes trying to keep up with the conversation! The man's eyes are rolling back in his head while the tidal wave of information is swallowing him up. When she is done, she feels better and he is overwhelmed. The conversation might look something like this:

> Honey, I was driving by your favorite truck store yesterday, you know the one where you got the cup holder? Right by your truck store is my favorite dress store, and there is the cutest suit in the window. It's my color—you know I went to that seminar on colors and I found out I was a "winter" so I knew if I got this suit you would say, "Oh Baby!" and I love that! You know the suit reminded me of the color of the gown the President's wife wore at the Inauguration Ball. She wore a different gown to every ball that night, but the one I remember was a yellow color—it was the same color as the racing suits those women wore in the Olympic speed ice skating. Remember honey, they were in all black with that yellow stripe on it and they looked so skinny. I think I should wear stripes more too. Remember that last skater? She fell right at the finish line. I thought, "How sad! She spent four years of her life training, and then she fell!" And that reminded me of our kids, going to high school this fall. What if our kids fall down in their faith? We should stop and pray for the kids.

And ladies, while you think your man is praying he is asking, "So what about my truck?"

The other characteristic that creates havoc in male-female interaction is the fact that most men have boxes that have no words. These boxes are just as blank as a white sheet of paper. They are empty! To help relieve stress in his life, he will "park" in these boxes to relax.

Amazingly, his wife seems to always notice when he is in park. She notices his blank look and the relaxed posture he has taken on the couch. She assumes this is a good time to talk since he is so relaxed and so she invariably asks, "What are you thinking, sweetheart?"

He immediately panics. Not wanting to disappoint his wife, his eyes start darting back and forth, hoping to find some box in close proximity that has words in it.

When a woman is stressed, she likes to talk her way through the situation. For example, when I am stressed, my mom knows it, my sister knows it, my best friend knows it, my prayer partner knows it—the clerk at the grocery store will know it! However, men process stress differently. When stress hits, a man also likes to escape to a favorite easy box to recharge. Most of these recharger boxes actually are shaped like boxes: the newspaper, TV and computer screen, the garage, basketball courts, the football field, the refrigerator—and the bed! These escapes all function like battery rechargers for men. If we give men time in the recharger, they will have energy to listen to us and carry life's responsibilities.

The Bible encourages us to "serve one another humbly in love" (Galatians 5:13). One of the ways Bill and I work this out in our marriage is to ask, "Who is this conversation for first?" Both the husband's and wife's needs usually cannot be met in the same conversation at the same time. I have found that if I allow Bill to recharge in one of his easy boxes, he is a much better listener when he returns. I also have found if I journal or pray through my feelings before God, Bill is not hit with the whole tsunami of my emotions and the conversation goes more smoothly.

If it's his turn to talk, practice staying in the box he wants to open. You see, when he brings up an issue for discussion, he actually intends to talk about that issue. The problem develops because you immediately recognize all the issues that are related to the one he brought up. Picture men with deep boxes. Their emotions are at the bottom of each box. If we stay focused on one topic and resist the urge to open up all the surrounding boxes, we buy our men the emotional time they need to work their way down through the layers of the box and we discover all their precious feelings. God had a great idea when he made us male and female—so *vive la différence!*

Differences in Pace

It is impossible to be involved with people and not be busy. So how do you figure out how busy you should be as a person (or a couple or a family)? It begins with finding your own personal pace as an individual. In Bill's book *The 10 Best Decisions a Man Can Make*, he shares an easy way to identify and evaluate your pace. It is based on 1 Corinthians 9:24: "Do you not know that in a race all the runners run, but only one receives the prize? So run that you may obtain it."

Every race has its own pace. Marathoners do not run their race at a sprinter's pace, or vice versa. We saw the practical side of knowing your pace when we were youth pastors and we led a bicycling trip down the California coastline. To help us all train, we had a professional cyclist come lead us all on a practice ride. The pro-cyclist explained that we each have a pace at which we can ride all day. If we ride faster than our natural pace, we tire easily. But if we ride slower than our natural pace, we can also become weary. Everyone has a pace at which they function best.

To help with the discussion, Bill created five categories, or vehicles, that describe the possibilities for the speed at which each of us can live: muscle car, sports car, semitruck, mail truck, and tractor. See if you can identify yourself and those you love.

The muscle car. These have big engines and are designed to go in a straight line with an abundance of pull and dramatic speed. This is the person who...

- likes to go fast and focus forward
- charges hard toward goals
- makes quick decisions and pursues big opportunities
- schedules activities that demand intensity and require her best effort
- easily grows restless

- can often be heard to say, "Let's go!"

The sports car. Some of you move more like sports cars. These vehicles are fun, agile, and quick. They prefer roads that have lots of turns and quick transitions. This is the person who…

- lives for the surprise around the next corner of life
- is most interested in new opportunities, experiences, and discoveries
- gets bored when there are no spontaneous activities
- unlike the muscle car, does not just want to go fast in just one direction, but in many directions at once
- loves variety

The semitruck. Some people operate in life more like a semitruck. This is the person who…

- starts and stops slow
- plans out and takes time to navigate course corrections
- can travel long distances at consistent speeds without a lot of variation
- maintains a steady and even pace
- doesn't move as fast as muscle cars and sports cars but can carry large amounts of responsibility
- faithfully plods along until the work is done
- is not spectacular or nimble but keeps the rest of us going
- forms the backbone of our communities, our organizations, and our churches

The mail truck. This is the person who has a sign on his back: "Makes Frequent Stops." This is the person who…

- is intensely interested in individuals

- finds life is consistently interrupted by conversations and projects to help people
- makes individuals feel important by being engaging and encouraging
- starts with energy and then stops to help
- eventually gets back on task but justifies the delay because others were helped

The tractor. Tractors are incredibly useful but they move slowly. This is the person who...

- fails to accomplish tasks when driven too fast
- is easy to follow and keep track of
- doesn't make sharp turns
- patiently waits for the strategic time
- tends to have one speed and works at that speed all day
- is often taken for granted but does some of the most important work on earth

Which of the five vehicles best represents the pace at which you like to live?

If you are married, share your response with your spouse and then listen to his answers. You might have to compromise as a couple and go at one person's pace at different times of the week or year. Decide at what pace you will run at when the entire family is functioning together. The vital task is to decide together how you'll function well within that pace.

By walking on love's path, I love God more, but I also find I
love myself, my life, and others more too.

CHAPTER 7

Becoming Productive

If you are a mother, or have ever babysat, chances are you have read the children's story *The Little Engine That Could*. The story chugs forward with an optimistic little engine who encouraged himself by saying, "I think I can, I think I can." In Philippians 4:13, the apostle Paul says, "I can do all this through him who gives me strength." Recite that verse to yourself. God has given us the resources to accomplish all He assigns to us.

The first seminar I ever gave was when I was a young mom, just under age thirty. I still have the notes for it: *On Track: Living a Balanced and Productive Life*. The photo on the front cover was of a set of railroad tracks leading to a vibrant sun. The feelings I wanted the women to have were hope, excitement, and confidence in the plan God would give them. That's the goal I still have for women in all my audiences, and for the women reading this book.

That seminar day started with me asking women to have a quiet time with Jesus and listen to the answers to a few questions to help them discover their unique calling or life passion. Having a laser focus on your calling makes all other decisions easier and more obvious. I have added more clarifying questions over the years. A little later in this chapter you'll be able to answer some of them for yourself. But first let's talk about how and why to discover your core purpose, mission, calling, passion—or whatever you want to call that sweet spot of being in the center of God's will.

On my personal stationery, I capture the heart of this sentiment with this verse:

> The Sovereign LORD is my strength; he makes my feet like
> the feet of a deer, he enables me to tread on the heights
> (Habakkuk 3:19).

I want to tread on the heights God has prepared for me—and I want that for you too!

Discover Your Destiny!

For me, discovering my calling and stepping into that calling was a several-year process, and I have found that to be the case for most women. Often this process begins during our university years because the educational system forces us to ask questions of ourselves to keep moving forward in achieving a degree. However, I have seen that living out your unique calling is not a "once and done" process. Rather, it should become a place we revisit at major transition points in life: when we graduate from high school, college, or graduate programs; when we fall in love and marry (or decide singleness is our call); when we become mothers; when our children get older and we find we have a little more time (or mental capacity) for interests outside the family; when our children become more independent as teens (or as we hit midlife and our minds and bodies adjust); and especially as our children launch and we find ourselves with an empty nest. Then, later, as our health may force us to slow our pace, we will make the last of the decisions on how to keep living out our calling until we hit the finish line of life and hear, "Well done, good and faithful servant."

As I was writing this last chapter, I took a break to be on a conference call with a woman I greatly admire, Jill Briscoe. She is an author and speaker and has served as a pastor's wife, a director of women's ministry, and a trailblazer for women worldwide. She is the founder of *Just Between Us*, a magazine for women in leadership, which she started when she was 54 years old—and at 80 she still travels the globe, often to war-torn or third-world countries, to train and encourage believers—and there is no sign of her stopping anytime soon! My usual greeting to her when I communicate is, "So where in the world does God have you today?"

No matter your age or season of life, whether you are at the trailhead, the middle of the journey, or nearer the end of the road, God still has a plan to use you—right up to your last breath.

Remember the story of Caleb from the Bible? When he was a young man, Caleb was one of the brave men who explored the Promised Land and returned with the news that it was inhabited by some tough people. But as a man of faith, Caleb agreed with God that Israel should go in and victory would be won. However, the fear of others won out.

Decades later, Joshua came to him with a request to join the battle for the Promised Land. This is Caleb's reply:

> Now then, just as the Lord promised, he has kept me alive for forty-five years since the time he said this to Moses, while Israel moved about in the wilderness. So here I am today, eighty-five years old! I am still as strong today as the day Moses sent me out; I'm just as vigorous to go out to battle now as I was then.

Each of you have a purpose that only you were designed to live out. He might not keep you young and strong like Caleb, but He'll equip you for the task He gives.

Same Box, Different Wrapping Paper

We are all given the same three items by God: time, talent, and treasure. We are all given the same amount of time, but it is up to us how we use it. We are all given some kind of talent, and when we begin a relationship with God, we are also bestowed a spiritual gift. While a case might be made that some people seem to have more talent than others, to God every person has the same value and the same responsibility to invest in whatever talents they have been given—no matter the number. Lastly, we are all given treasure, or the ability to earn an income. Again, sometimes people think others are given a bit of a head start in life if they come from a family with money, but a silver spoon isn't always an advantage.

> What you are is God's gift to you.
> What you become is your gift to God.
> —Hans Urs von Balthasar

Recently while watching *The Shark Tank*, a TV show where budding entrepreneurs make presentations to millionaires in hopes of securing some investment money, I heard one shark say she never invests in the companies started by rich kids. They are not as "hungry" to make a go of it because they have a financial safety net. She made a case that more moguls created success out of their last (or first) hundred dollars. If they didn't produce or sell, they went hungry, living in their car or on the street.

What Is Success?

> Success is liking yourself, liking what you do,
> and liking how you do it.
> —Maya Angelou

It is prudent to pause and ask yourself, "What is success to me?" We traveled to the Philippines to do missions work, and we were heartbroken by the poverty we saw. But the Filipino people were some of the most generous and happy people we had ever met! After a week with our hosts, we complimented this wonderful trait of perpetual optimism. And the response has stayed with us. "Many in our country see our children as our heritage; we see our hard work and kind servant spirit as our gift to the world. Some in the world might pity us for our lack of money, but we are wealthy in relationships, happiness, and love."

There are many ways to evaluate what treasure is and how to

accumulate various kinds of wealth and prosperity. It is important for you to spend time with God and define happiness, success, and prosperity in your own heart.

We All Need to Eat

Scripture does give a baseline on what is provision and who should provide:

> Give me neither poverty nor riches, but give me only my daily bread. Otherwise, I may have too much and disown you and say, "Who is the LORD?" Or I may become poor and steal, and so dishonor the name of my God (Proverbs 30:8-9).

> The one who is unwilling to work shall not eat (2 Thessalonians 3:10).

We all are called to contribute—in some capacity—toward our own life. While there are a few, due to severe physical or mental hardship, who are unable to provide for themselves, my guess is that if you are reading this book, you have a measure of ability to contribute.

Money is a fuel. It is like gas for your car. It gets you where you believe God wants you to go. One principle I have learned is, "If God calls, God funds." Now the methods by which God funds and the timing of when He funds…that is the place where your faith and your ability to follow God's leading are most vital.

As women, we should be wise stewards of our resources. My friend Ellie Kay is a family finance expert, and I asked her to simplify her wealth of financial wisdom into some quick bits of advice:

Ten Tips for Women to Make Better Financial Choices

1. Avoid emotional spending. Never shop online or in the store when you are depressed or lonely because you are far more likely to engage in "shopping therapy" and overspend.

2. Show love through actions, not things. If you have a love language of gift giving or if you tend to show love to others by what you buy for them, shift your point of view and save your budget in the process.

3. Volunteer often. Those who have the best balanced financial lives understand how fortunate they are by helping those who are less fortunate.

4. Err on the side of generosity. By tithing ten percent of your income, you invite God's blessing upon your money matters and live a more abundant financial life. If you are going to err, don't let it be on the side of stinginess.

5. Distinguish between needs and wants. Most of us do not have unlimited financial resources. Ask yourself if every purchase is a need or a want. You can say it's a "want" and buy it anyway, but if you do that on a regular basis, you'll live an unhealthy, materialistic life.

6. Play the waiting game. In order to avoid impulse buying, when you see something on sale in the mall or online, wait 24 hours to purchase it. This helps you get beyond the impulse to see if it's something you truly need.

7. Have a money buddy. Accountability is a wonderful thing. Every woman should have a person who can ask you the hard questions about sticking to your budget, paying down consumer debt, or funding retirement. In community, you are far more likely to keep your financial commitments toward good stewardship.

8. Become a master saver. Read money saving blogs, download apps for coupon codes, and be prepared to negotiate on goods and services.

9. Negotiate. Whether you are negotiating the price of a car or the bid on painting your house, you have to feel it's the best deal for you. Tell the seller, "I don't feel comfortable with that price," and then be quiet. Nine out of ten times

I'll get a counterbid I feel more comfortable with, and if I don't, I feel the freedom to walk away.

10. Pray about money matters. Even a financial expert like myself needs to pray to make wise financial decisions, that people won't be able to take financial advantage of me, and that I'll be able to find the best provision for my budget. When in doubt, pray.[1]

Time

Everyone has 365 days each year and 24 hours in those days. Take out time to sleep, shower, exercise, and eat, and you've still got 12 hours each day to make a wonderful impact, leave your imprint, and spread your positive influence! That is plenty of time to get some of your hopes, dreams, and adventures done!

So let's look closer at how you spend those 12 hours. The average woman spends five hours a day watching TV[2] and four hours a day on Facebook.[3] She spends 54 minutes a day getting dressed, doing her hair and putting on her makeup.[4] If she works, the average commute is 25 minutes. Here's the challenge: can you shave any of this time down for other endeavors? Maybe skip all (or most) of the TV and Facebook time, or perhaps multitask by doing household tasks while watching media. Get your social media time down to an hour a day or less. Can you trim your morning prep time to under 30 minutes by planning your wardrobe ahead of schedule and making hair style decisions in advance?

Just think what you could do with that extra time! You could take a longer quiet time with God so you could mature spiritually. You could enroll in a class to learn a new skill. If you can listen to audiobooks on your commute or while exercising, you will gain a few more hours back each day too.

Maybe those extra hours could be spent on relationships—socializing with friends, volunteering in your community or church, connecting with your spouse or significant other, or doing something with or for your children. Perhaps you are ready for a career change. Those hours gained could go toward being mentored to start your own business or running a part-time business from home. They could be used for a stress-reducing activity like art, painting, pottery, or photography.

It's not enough to be busy, so are the ants.
The question is, what are we busy about?

—Henry David Thoreau

If you are serious about shifting your time priorities, keep a time journal for a month to spot time wasters. I like to picture my life like a plate or a pie chart. I want to know what percentage of my life is spent on each of my priorities. After you tally where you spend your hours, input that data into your computer using a pie chart that shows where your time was spent.

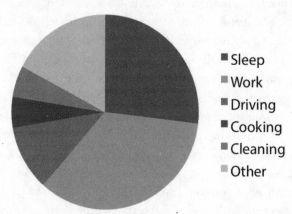

Then simply ask, "Am I happy with how I use my time?" If you are, well done, keep moving forward in that healthy pattern. If not, ask, "What do I need to do less of and what do I want to do more of?" Then set goals to have your daily life reflect your heart. It might take a few years to get there, but whittle away at the changes a little at a time and eventually you will love your life.

It took me eight years to get my BA. I pushed pause on my studies and worked to help my husband earn his BA and then his Mdiv. I had three babies between semesters of college, but eventually I wore the cap and gown. If you whittle away on a dream, even a little at a time, eventually you will reach your goal!

Time Saving Tips

My friend Marcia Ramsland is the Organizing Pro. She wrote the book on home organization—literally! Her organizing wisdom has blessed me over and again. She says, "The faster the pace of your life, the more organized you need to be. Excellent personal habits can save you a lot of time and distraction. And good time habits can give you the time you need to get things done."

Let's start with Ten Time Saving Tips for every day:

1. Make your bed *every* morning. It only takes two minutes to give you 16 hours of order while you carry on your day. You will be uplifted to come back to a beautiful, restful room at the end of the day. And your room is half clean once you do it!

2. Practice the "Two Minute Pickup" every time you leave a room or your desk. That is, turn around and quickly put away everything for two minutes. The less you have to put away, the less fragmented your life will be when you return.

3. Learn to love clean counters. Significant amounts of time are saved if keys, glasses, important papers, shoes, and clutter are neatly put away or tossed. Don't leave piles of flyers, coupons, and projects sitting out.

4. Cut your work in half by putting things away *now* instead of putting them down to come back to later. One of the biggest time wasters is to say, "I'll deal with that later." (And when would that be?) Put everything away now!

5. Set the pace for your day by arriving early or at least on time at your first event or appointment. Have you ever

noticed that your arrival time at the first event sets the pace for the rest of your day?

6. Most people go to sleep the same number of hours after dinner, so make sure dinner is early and regular. You'll save time during the day if you commit yourself to getting enough sleep and waking up rested.

7. Decide if "To Do" items you write down are "Intentions" or "Commitments." If they are commitments to really get done, assign them a specific calendar day and do them. If they are intentions, cross them off your list and quit rewriting unreasonably long lists over and over.

8. Write every action on a day or on a master list under sections titled, "To Do," "To Call," "Errands," "Work," and "Personal." Don't clutter your mind with things to remember. Write them down in your planner.

9. Strive to focus your day's events on things you enjoy. You will unconsciously sabotage your time if you have too many stressful things to do.

10. Congratulate yourself every day for the things you do accomplish. If you go through your daily activities with a smile and good attitude, you get bonus points![5]

Talent

Every woman has a talent and when she connects to the God who created her, the spiritual gift placed inside her is awakened. Here is a list of possible Spiritual Gifts I have compiled and simplified over the years to help women identify the gifts she could possibly have been given by God. Many churches and ministries offer online inventories to help you identify your top gifts. However, the best way to really pinpoint your gifts is to try them out! If you are left energized and enthused to use it again and the people you ministered to were helped, that gift is likely a great fit!

- Administration: directing projects.
- Craftsmanship and artistry: using your hands to create or build so that others are pointed toward God.
- Evangelism: communicating spiritual truth to lead someone to a personal relationship with God.
- Exhortation: encouraging people and walking alongside them to bring out the best in them.
- Giving: providing faithful stewardship and sharing with others.
- Help and serving: caring for others by working behind the scenes.
- Hospitality: using the home or other resources to make people feel included and welcomed.
- Intercession: devoting time and energy to pray more than the average person does.
- Knowledge: sharing information that helps people live life in a productive, healthy manner.
- Leadership: directing people.
- Mercy: showing compassion and acting to meet needs.
- Music: singing or playing instruments to turn hearts toward God.
- Prophecy: publicly proclaiming truth.
- Teaching: explaining harder concepts to others and helping them apply them.
- Wisdom: applying knowledge with discretion and insight.
- Writing: communicating information to help others grow in faith, develop life skills, or turn toward God.

It is vital that you become self-aware. Jesus made it clear that we are to invest the talents we are given so that God is glorified, people's lives are improved, and Kingdom priorities are carried forward. He shared his heart for people becoming all God intended in the parable of the talents:

> It will be like a man going on a journey, who called his servants and entrusted his wealth to them. To one he gave five bags of gold…Then he went on his journey. The man who had received five bags of gold went at once and put his money to work and gained five bags more…
>
> After a long time the master of those servants returned and settled accounts with them. The man who had received five bags of gold brought the other five. "Master," he said, "you entrusted me with five bags of gold. See, I have gained five more."
>
> His master replied, "Well done, good and faithful servant! You have been faithful with a few things; I will put you in charge of many things. Come and share your master's happiness!"…For whoever has will be given more, and they will have an abundance (Matthew 25:14-29).

Invest your gifts, abilities, talents, skills, time, treasure—anything you have—because God wants us all to be wise stewards to the best of our ability. And when we maximize our skill set, God rewards us by entrusting us with more responsibilities. More people to shepherd, more skills to implement, more treasure to multiply, and more vision of what could be made a reality!

> Give, and it will be given to you. A good measure, pressed down, shaken together and running over, will be poured into your lap. For with the measure you use, it will be measured to you (Luke 6:38).

We Each Have Our Part

One of my favorite stories my husband preaches is of the Disciples' Catering Business. Here it is in his words.

In Luke 9, the disciples participated with Jesus in a day-long crusade. They taught the crowds, healed the sick, and ministered to the masses. Late in the afternoon, the disciples began to realize a problem was brewing. Five thousand men had brought their families, and nobody had eaten all day. They were trying to be helpful, so they approached their rabbi: "Send the crowd away so they can go to the surrounding villages and countryside and find food and lodging, because we are in a remote place here" (verse 12).

The next statement is shocking. Jesus replied, "You give them something to eat."

The disciples had no food, no animals, and no place to go shopping. They had nothing to work with, and yet Jesus told them to solve the problem. The adventure was on. The men now had a challenge to work on that was way beyond their abilities. They had two options. They could retreat from the challenge in defeat or they could face the challenge head on and see what God did with it.

I am sure they felt overwhelmingly inadequate. I am sure they brainstormed among themselves ways to address the need. I am sure they concluded they were going to need Jesus's help in a big way if these people were going to get even a measly snack, let alone a meal.

Jesus called, so they decided to take a run at it...They scrambled around and finally came up with five loaves of bread and two fish. They had the equivalent of two lunches with 12,000 to 15,000 people to feed. The need is huge. The resources are scarce. The adventure is about to get large.

I believe this is where most of us live...We entertain...lofty goals. [However], our evaluation of our talents and resources leaves only one conclusion: The need is way bigger than my ability, and yet God has called me to this. If Jesus doesn't get involved here, intensely involved, failure is guaranteed...They knew they didn't have enough. Jesus knew they didn't have enough. A kindergartener would have known they didn't have enough. But it was all they had.

The difference was that Jesus had called them out to do this, and so it was part of the great adventure He had for them. Jesus took their scant resources and added His abundant resources to them. In the end, everyone ate until they were satisfied, and every disciple collected a basket of leftovers.

Our resources are simply the starting investment that proves we have accepted the challenge. What drives the adventure in our lives are the resources of Jesus that make us "more than conquerors" (Romans 8:37) and overcomers (1 John 4:4)...We cannot do it on our own, but we dare not run from it because it is how God works in our lives.[6]

Psalm 37:40 tells us, "The Lord helps [the righteous] and delivers them; he delivers them from the wicked and saves them, because they take refuge in him." Did you notice the prerequisite for being delivered? "Take refuge in him." This means we are looking to God for leadership, help, and provision. We are willing to obey His leading and do our part. There are numerous examples in the Bible of God coming through when His people did their part.

God fed, but His people had to pick up the quail and manna.

God led by cloud and fire, but His people had to do the walking.

God conquered, but His people had to march and blow trumpets.

God gave victory, but His people had to go to war with pots and pitchers.

God parted the waters, but His people had to step in.

God freed, but His people had to walk out of their jail cell.

God gave in abundance, but His people had to cast their nets.

God raised the dead, but His people had to roll away the stone.

God delivered, but Rahab had to hang out the red cord.

God provided, but Naomi had to go home, and Ruth had to go to the fields.

God brought whole households to faith, but Lydia, a busy business woman had to go to the river, listen, and open her home for a church plant.

God sent the Messiah to save the world, but Mary had to carry the child in her womb for nine months.

Who's doing the work here? God. All we have to do is respond.

Create a Compass

The more you have to give, the more people want from you, so you need a personal compass by which you make vital choices and decisions. It is easy to fall into a pattern of doing the urgent thing first, oiling the squeaky wheels, and putting out fires. So what tools can protect our emotional and spiritual well-being—as well as protecting our marriage and family?

I have a compass that sits on my desk. It was given to me by a seasoned women's ministry director and pastor's wife. When she gave it to me, she said, "May you hear God's voice above all others. May God's call and God's Word be the compass to your heart and life."

I began to ask myself, "How can I create an inner compass? How can I stay facing 'true north' on the path and plan God has for me, my marriage, and my family?" And God began to layer the answers in my heart.

I have compressed and simplified the key tools that have helped us know God's plan and path for us, and they will help you gain that "compass for life" too!

The Mission

In seminary, we went to a marriage conference before the first semester began. Dr. Norm Wright challenged us to write a personal mission statement and a marriage mission. As undergrads, Bill and I had each written our own simple personal mission statement, but as newlyweds, we felt a need to dovetail our missions and create a unified vision for marriage. Here is our marriage and family mission statement:

> We, Bill and Pam Farrel, have a desire to fulfill the Great Commission through using our skills in professional ministry, with a focus of using the communication gifts God

has given us. We are committed to personal discipleship as a lifestyle. We want our home to be an oasis where those who enter can see Christ at work in our marriage and family and where they can find hope. We, the Farrels, are committed to fun and friendships. We value people more than things. We prefer memories over material goods. We are committed to raising our children in such a way as they have the opportunity to know the benefits of personally knowing Jesus and walking with Him. We are committed to helping them discover their talents and equipping them to help fulfill the Great Commission and to have fun and a fulfilling life while doing so.

Clarifying Questions

God made you unique. You were designed to live at this time in history for a reason. In Jeremiah 1:5 God tells us, "Before I formed you in the womb I knew you, before you were born I set you apart; I appointed you as a prophet to the nations." You too have a mission.

Here are a few quick questions to get you started thinking about what should be in your personal mission statement:

- What do you LOVE doing?
- What makes you feel more yourself?
- What do others compliment you for doing?
- What is unique about you? (To discover your uniqueness, journal about times you felt God use you. Now reread them. Are there any common attributes? Same people group? Same experiences? Same giftedness? Look for God's repeating patterns in your life.)
- What do you think about before bed and early in the morning when the house is quiet?
- What was the last issue that made you righteously angry or brought you to tears?
- What or who are you willing to die for?

- What or who are you willing to go to jail for if the need arose?

- What or who are you willing to be inconvenienced for?

- What do you talk about the most?

- What are your core values?

- What legacy do you want to leave after you have left this earth?

- What do you want written on your tombstone?

- If you were guaranteed success and had unlimited funds, what would you want to do for God?

- Do you have a favorite verse?

Then dovetail your heart with your husband's as you pen a marriage mission statement by answering a few extra questions:

- As a couple, what do you love?

- As a couple, what are you great at when you team up?

- What kinds of things are you complimented on as a team?

- What is your family known for?

- What is the legacy you want to pass on to your children and grandchildren?

- Do you have a verse that captures your love?

- Do you have a saying or a verse that captures your passion or calling as a couple or family?

Using the answers to the above questions as clues, see if you can create a mission statement that sums up why you think God has placed you together. You might begin with words like…

We believe we are called to…

To fulfill God's call on our lives, we hereby declare…

We found that it took several rough drafts to hone our mission. We discovered the best place to work on it was in the car driving on vacations or family outings. A personal mission will direct your own life, but it can also be used by God to direct you to your life partner. As we were teamed together as a couple and then as a family, we seemed to be able to focus on the long-term goals we had for our marriage, our family, and then for our ministry—in that strategic order. Life works better when we all keep this order of priorities in mind.

Every time you make a choice you are turning
the central part of you, the part that chooses,
into something a little different than what it was before.

—C.S. Lewis

One of the most powerful reasons to have a personal mission as well as a marriage and family mission is to keep your identity intact in the hectic pace of life. It also helps you in vital decision-making situations, and most importantly, it protects your kids because they will have a strong family identity. "The single most important thing you can do for your family may be the simplest of all: develop a strong family narrative," says Bruce Feiler, author of *The Secrets of Happy Families*. In an article for *The New York Times*, he shares this insightful research:

> The more children knew about their family's history, the stronger their sense of control over their lives, the higher their self-esteem and the more successfully they believed their families functioned...

> Jim Collins, a management expert and author of "Good to Great," told me that successful human enterprises of any kind, from companies to countries, go out of their way to capture their core identity. In Mr. Collins's terms, they "preserve core, while stimulating progress." The same applies to families, he said.

> Mr. Collins recommended that families create a mission statement similar to the ones companies and other organizations use to identify their core values.[7]

We can share our family story from the past—lessons learned, accomplishments gained, obstacles overcome—as well as cast a vision of what God is calling our family to become through developing a family mission. A mission keeps us living in clear focus of our calling and trains our kids to do the same.

While it is possible to memorize a mission statement, a short motto will more easily stick in your mind—and in your children's hearts. Make your mission a bit more memorable by summing it up into a catchy phrase like you might print on a T-shirt, coffee mug, or bumper sticker. Our family motto is a paraphrase of a favorite verse:

Those who honor God, God honors (1 Samuel 2:30).

Before I make a decision, I match it up next to the family motto to see if it does indeed "honor God."

Moniker

Make it visual! What symbol reflects where you are going?

One friend of ours adopted a sunflower as her symbol because a sunflower moves throughout the day so its face is always toward the sun. She wanted to be a woman who always had her face toward the Son of God.

A colleague had a photo framed of herself atop California's highest mountain peak because her ministry is to help others reach their peak potential.

Here is a drawing of our family crest:

Our symbol was created when Bill was a youth pastor and we were praying about what we wanted for our children. In short, we wanted our children to be *Learners and Leaders who Love God.* The two interconnected hearts symbolize our commitment to keep our promises—especially in relationships. The cross with the star means that we believe each person has a God-given passion or calling and when we are in correct relationship with God, He empowers us to reach our potential.

Creating a symbol can be as simple as designing a crest or emblem with pictures that answer this question: *What are four things you want said about you at your funeral?* Place a symbol for each word or trait in each section of the crest below, and then post this on your desk or bathroom mirror as inspiration.

So what is the long-term result of clearly specifying your mission and designing ways to remember it? Bill and I are happily married and have traversed through numerous ministry career roles in our 35 years together. All three of our sons love and serve God, and the two who are married fell in love with beautiful women who also love God. Both these sons have written marriage mission statements to guide their own families. Yes, we have fruit from our ministry, but the sweetest fruit is the legacy we are leaving in our children and grandchildren.

These are the tools that create the inner compass that can guide your life, your love, and your legacy.

Each day we choose to live the legacy we want to leave.

Dreams with Deadlines

In my twenties, I drew a set of stairs that showed how I was stepping up into the adventure God had for me as a writer, speaker, and leader. I like the stairstep visual because it helps us see the progress we are making. Here is the process:

1. Write the big dream or adventure in a sentence. *With God's help, I want to*_____. What would go in the blank on your page? What do you want to achieve?

2. Break down that big goal into smaller goals. What things do you need to do to get you to that end result? You might have to do some investigation to make your action item list. Talk to mentors who have achieved that goal. Read blogs and books or take a course to get equipped. Watch videos or listen to audio training. In fact, "Investigate options" could be your Step 1.

3. Number your list into the chronological order you think best. Make a plan to reach the top of your stairway.

4. Assign a deadline to each item on your list (and a rule of thumb is things will usually take twice as long and cost twice as much as you might think!).

5. Write the goal, then write the deadline for each goal on each of the stairs. You now have your Stair Step to Success Action Plan.

Goals are just dreams with deadlines!
—Emilie Barnes[8]

Target
Date: Goal:

Often people asked how I found time to write 40 books in twenty years, have a vibrant ministry as a Women's Director, and create a healthy marriage and a loving positive home for our children. I always rephrase their inquiry with my answer:

I didn't find the time, I made the time.

Here are seven simple steps for creating time to **PRODUCE** the desired outcome. You will be more productive and achieve more if you can accomplish these.

1. *Plan out the future.* Plan each year, each month, each week, each day, and each hour. Those who fail to prepare, prepare to fail. I color-code my calendar so I can find items for family, work, and social life quickly on my schedule, and I input all important details with each calendar entry. Experiment with various planning systems, software, and apps to find ones that work for your life and personality. I also plan how I can delegate tasks to my kids, volunteers, or employees. If someone else can do it almost as well as me, I delegate it! I try to keep tasks and priorities that need my personal focus, energy, and attention.

2. *Respond instead of reacting.* I don't waste time on negative emotions. Worry, self-doubt, and frustration over delays or plans gone awry are time wasters. If I hit a really hard emotional hurdle, I will cry for a few minutes and then plan a time to better deal with the emotional fallout later over coffee with a friend or mentor, a counseling session, or a heart-to-heart talk with my husband. To keep a positive disposition, I also plan in nourishing days off, time out for favorite activities, dates with my husband, and days off for solitude and serenity. By cordoning off time for self-care, I gain time. I protect my heart and mind, so it takes a pretty sizeable trauma to unravel me emotionally.

3. *Optimize multitasking.* Multitasking doesn't always make us more efficient. However, if one of the tasks requires very little brainpower, I find I can link them. For example, I can walk and listen to podcasts or audio books; I can fold laundry and watch the news; I can do my morning stretches while I listen to worship songs; I can walk to the beach and pray through priorities; I can dust or do dishes

while memorizing Scripture; I can walk on a treadmill at a
slow pace and make a phone call or post to social media.

4. ***Delegate tasks for efficiency.*** Why waste time doing it all
   alone? It's time to stop thinking you're the only one who
   can get a task done right. Ask others to come alongside
   and lend a hand *before* you start feeling overwhelmed.
   Tap into their gifts for service, leadership, or organization.
   You'll all be celebrating the joy of partnership!

5. ***Use every minute.*** I never just wait around. If I have an
   extra few minutes I check e-mail or read newsletters, a
   magazine article, or a book (usually a nonfiction book that
   can help me improve some area of my life). I also handle
   small household tasks in those random five- to ten-minute
   slots: I can clean out a drawer, wipe down the kitchen, or
   empty the dishwasher. I might also call or text one of my
   family members or friends a quick encouragement. I see
   every minute as a precious gift.

6. ***Calendar priorities first.*** I carve out time with God,
   marriage getaways and date nights, and our kids' major
   responsibilities, activities, and celebrations. These all
   get placed on the calendar as far out as we can possibly
   manage to place them there. I also schedule into my
   planner my goal and the time it will take to achieve the
   desired outcome. This process doesn't result in pulling off
   the perfect plan—no one can control life's unpredictable
   variables—but it does produce progress toward the most
   important memory makers and priorities. I plan, then
   I flex: *Blessed are the flexible for they shall not be broken.*
   When your priorities are clear, it is easier to recalculate and
   regroup quickly.

7. ***Elevate your vision.*** I want to keep a more heavenly
   perspective so I pray. I get God's viewpoint on my life,
   my marriage, my family, my ministry, my business, my

friendships, my health—on all my life. I have found it saves me time to do life God's way. Any time I spend in prayer, Bible reading, listening to Bible teaching, or being in a Bible study group, God always seems to multiply back to me. The bestselling book title of Bill Hybels, pastor of one of America's megachurches, says it best: *Too Busy Not to Pray.*

What are your dreams? Wake up and put goals to them, and set a course of action to achieve some of those dreams!

Off Track Attack

The *Alamosa Journal* captured the horror of a train going off its tracks:

> Train No. 11, the Missouri Pacific flyer, crashed through a bridge over an arroya…It is estimated that of the 125 passengers on board the ill-fated train between eighty and one hundred lost their lives…Water was flowing over a trestle when the train struck it. The engine got almost across, but fell back, and baggage car, smoker and chair cars plunged into the torrent…Wreckage is visible in all directions.[9]

Going off the rails brought death and destruction. In the same way, if our lives go off the rails of God's plan, the results can be devastating. In all my years of working with women, I've found that nothing gets us off track faster, or with greater long-term consequences, than our unwillingness to run our relationships according to God's plan.

Rails keep a train going safely toward a destination. God's plans for relationships are the tracks keeping our lives moving ahead safely too. If you are on an open prairie, you can plainly see the parallel tracks for miles, but as in the case above, a flash flood covered the tracks, derailing the train. Satan loves to do that to our relationships. The devil likes things to be confusing, in turmoil, sin mucking up the rails and the lines so blurred that you get off track and derail your life.

Blurred Lines was a song that shot to the top of the charts when it first released in 2013. The explicit song depicts a man's desire to turn a "good girl" into some sexual play toy. The relationship portrayed is not anything close to a healthy one from a biblical worldview. However, it has a catchy tune, so people play it in the backgrounds of their lives and hum along, not even realizing that if they were to mimic the song their lives would get off track in a hurry.

In today's "don't judge me" and "don't tell me what to do" moral climate, people are comfortable when lines are blurred because then there is no accountability—there are no tracks. People embrace the blurry lines as long as it seems to be going well for them...but the problem with blurry lines is that in a relationship, blurry lines hurt everyone. When the train goes off the tracks, disaster, death, and destruction follow.

But God's plans aren't blurry. God is very specific on what works to keep a relationship on track, happy, and healthy. Let's review a familiar passage in the Amplified Bible translation. The additional meanings, captured in the parentheses in the paragraph below, create a working definition of what God was intending in the way we treat one another in relationships:

> For this is the will of God, that you should be consecrated (separated and set apart for pure and holy living): that you should abstain *and* shrink from all sexual vice, that each one of you should know how to possess (control, manage) his own body in consecration (purity, separated from things profane) and honor, not [to be used] in the passion of lust like the heathen, who are ignorant of the true God *and* have no knowledge of His will, that no man transgress and overreach his brother *and* defraud him in this matter *or* defraud his brother in business. For the Lord is an avenger in all these things, as we have already warned you solemnly *and* told you plainly. For God has not called us to impurity but to consecration [to dedicate ourselves to the most thorough purity]. Therefore whoever disregards (sets aside and rejects this) disregards not man but God, Whose [very] Spirit [Whom] He gives to you is holy (chaste, pure) (1 Thessalonians 4:3–8 AMP).

God makes it abundantly clear that any form of sexual expression prior to a covenant marital commitment is not His plan for individuals, and any breech of your vows is also a clearly immoral choice. But the question we get most often is, *Why maintain the line?* Why maintain purity and abstinence prior to marriage and faithful fidelity after you say *I do?* Because God sees your body, my body, *every* body as precious and of high value. We are called to live life consecrated, dedicated to God—the maker of sexuality, the creator of our minds, bodies, souls, and spirits. It is *because* you are so valuable that the tracks were put in place to keep you safe.

If you stay within the tracks—within God's parameters for healthy relationships and sexuality—you'll experience the blessings God intended.

God gave us sex for five reasons:

- Procreation. "Be fruitful and increase in number" (Genesis 1:22).

- Recreation. "Isaac was sporting with Rebekah his wife" (Genesis 26:8 KJV).

- Reconnection. "Do not deprive each other except perhaps by mutual consent and for a time, so that you may devote yourselves to prayer. Then come together again" (1 Corinthians 7:5).

- Rejuvenation. "Strengthen me with raisins, refresh me with apples, for I am faint with love" (Song of Songs 2:5).

- Proclamation. "'For this reason a man will leave his father and mother and be united to his wife, and the two will become one flesh.' This is a profound mystery—but I am talking about Christ and the church" (Ephesians 5:31-32).

These are the tracks, the guardrails, of love. So in living a life in accordance to God's path, it really comes down to two familiar questions: Do you believe God loves you? Do you believe God truly, deep down loves you? Do you believe God is crazy about you? Do you believe He is thrilled with the beautiful amazing creation of *you*?

And then turn that question around:

Do you love God? Do you truly love, adore, honor, respect, and stand in awe of the God who created you and died on the cross to set you free? Do you believe God wants to keep you living in that fulfilling freedom so you can live in blessing on earth and in eternity?

If you believe God loves you, then you must also believe God wants the very best for you and your life, right? Then trust the love of God by honoring and obeying the relationship tracks He set in place—for your good, for the good of others you will be in relationship with, and for the good of society.

God's love protects and provides for everyone
involved in relationships.

How Can We Maintain God's Love Lines?

I have spelled out the principles found in the First Thessalonians passage and a few others in an easy-to-remember way. The tracks spell *LOVE*.

Live away from the temptation. First Corinthians 6:18 instructs us to "Flee from sexual immorality. All other sins a person commits are outside the body, but whoever sins sexually, sins against their own body." Remember the old children's Sunday school song? "Oh be careful little eyes what you see…" Be mindful about what you're putting into your mind, what you allow yourself to say, and the places you allow yourself to go.

Own your own body. First Thessalonians 4:4 reminds us that "each of you should learn to control your own body in a way that is holy and honorable." Before marriage, know what lights your passion so you can control it to bless your future. After marriage, know what unleashes your passions so you can focus it on your own husband.

Vigilantly protect others. First Thessalonians 4:5 reminds us not to live "in passionate lust like the pagans, who do not know God." Married or single, your choices are an expression of your love for God. Protect those you love by not trespassing into territory that is not yours. Don't step over another person's comfort line or go beyond the commitment level of your relationship. Don't exploit another person for your indulgence or selfish desires. And always consider the other person's relationship with God and their future happiness.

Evaluate all choices through the lens of eternity. First Thessalonians 4:8 finishes its instruction by saying, "Anyone who rejects this instruction does not reject a human being but God, the very God who gives you his Holy Spirit."

A large majority of the pain people experience can be traced back to going off track in relationships. God will allow legal and natural consequences of wrongdoing. If we choose not to love ourselves like God loves us, we will continue to not love ourselves and we will place ourselves further and further away from the heart and presence of God. At death, we will pay the consequences of our choices.

Choice 1: We do *not* love ourselves as God loves us and we do *not* love God. We distance ourselves from God's love so we will not sense or experience the blessings of the love of God here on earth, and God gives us the logical outcome of being separated from His love for eternity.

Choice 2: We *do* love ourselves as God loves us and we *do* express that love in our actions. We live in close friendship with God and we sense and experience God's hand of blessing on our lives and our love relationships.

Choice 3: We recognize when we get off track and we do not want to experience anymore negative consequences...so we do something about it! We make things right with God and God helps us make things right with others. God redeems the unhealthy choices and gives us a clear path to make future healthy choices. Eventually we will see the positive fruit of those healthy "back on track" choices both in this life and the one to come.

I will give you a new heart and put a new spirit in you; I
will remove from you your heart of stone and give you a
heart of flesh. And I will put my Spirit in you and move
you to follow my decrees and be careful to keep my laws.
Then…you will be my people, and I will be your God (Eze-
kiel 36:26-28).

The God who helped Israel gain a soft heart toward God is the same
God who can renew your heart and mine. When your heart matches
God's heart, your life becomes strong and secure because your future is
bonded to the Solid Rock, the God who cannot be shaken!

By walking on love's path, I love God more, but I also find I
love myself, my life, and others more too.

Back On Track

Whether in the area of relationships or another part of life, no one is
going to be 100 percent perfect. Right now, embrace the fact that somewhere your humanity will show up. Even when we try our best, we are
not going to be flawless. We will fail. It is how we handle our sins, frail-
ties, and failures that dictates how well we will be able to keep it together.

When you fail, don't run away.
Run to God.

We must become adept at not just learning to avoid falling, but also
learning to get back up and walk forward wiser. When we see a lapse in
our integrity, we should push pause and ask, "Why did this happen?"

If we are honest with ourselves, it can be traced back to a break-
down in one of those same two loves:

God's love toward me: What character trait of the God who loves
me am I forgetting?

My love toward God: How have I forgotten to give my worship and praise to God?

A preschooler was being enrolled by his father into school from being on the mission field with his family. When the teacher realized the dad was a spiritual leader, she asked, "Will you come to my class and explain the true meaning of Easter?"

The man agreed and went into the preschool classroom and asked, "Who knows the meaning of Easter?"

His own son piped up, "Easter is the day Jesus came down and died on the cross for our sins. You know, the bad things we say, do, or think. Then they put Him in a tomb. When He comes out of His tomb, if He sees His shadow, we have six more weeks of winter!"

Misperceptions, faulty images, and flawed or missing knowledge of God's character mixed with our own propensity for selfishness and sin can create the perfect environment for a misstep in our own integrity.

When our view of God is warped, sin is easier to justify. If a woman cheats, lies, or steals, she has forgotten that God is the all-knowing, all-powerful, sovereign ruler who calls Himself Truth. If she believed God was Truth, then she would seek to tell the truth. If she believed God knows all, is in control, and has the power over all, then she wouldn't need to manipulate, cut corners, or plot to deceive to gain an advantage.

Years ago, each time I would hit a tough circumstance I'd search for a verse to encourage me. Pages in my Bible became highlighted with verses that gave strength, hope, or comfort. However, after a move to a new city, I found myself lonely and depressed. But instead of reaching for my Bible, I called a friend. Mary pointed me back in the right direction, as only a best friend can do, and she asked me a pointed question:

What attribute of God are you forgetting? What trait of
Christ are you not believing?

Her words challenged me. I knew that I needed to get a fresh view of the God I loved and who loved me. I pulled out my marked-up Bible, strung together the verses, and personalized God's Word to my heart. It is really a message from God's heart to my own. Since that time, these verses have encouraged me to step out, try the improbable, and believe God for the impossible. No matter how dismal or overwhelming the circumstance, by reading verses like these, life is put in proper perspective.

God's very character can elevate you out of the pit. This letter now hangs in my home to remind me daily of who God is and of His personal love to me. Below is my letter, His Word personalized for me and you:

Dearest Child of Mine,

Nothing is impossible for Me. I am able to do immeasurably more than all you can ask or think. In Me all things were created, in heaven and on earth, visible and invisible, thrones, powers, rulers, authorities. All things were created by Me. I am before all things and in Me all things hold together.

Mine is the greatness and the power and the glory and the majesty and the splendor. I am exalted as head over all. Wealth and honor come from Me. In My hands are strength and power to exalt. Nothing on earth is My equal!

It is not by [your] might nor by [your] power but by My spirit. I know when you sit down and when you rise; I perceive your thoughts from afar. I am familiar with all your ways. Before a word is on your tongue I know it completely. You cannot flee from My presence. If you go up to the heavens, I am there; if you make your bed in the depths, I am there. If you rise on the wings of the dawn, if you settle on the far side of the sea, even there My hand will guide you, My right hand will hold you fast. Even the darkness is as light to Me.

I stretch out the heavens like a canopy and spread them out like a tent to dwell in. I measure the waters of the earth in the hollow of My hand, and with the breadth of My hand I mark off the heavens.

I am the Creator. I am the Wonderful Counselor, the Mighty God, the Everlasting Father, the Prince of Peace. I am the Alpha and Omega, the Beginning and the End.

I am immortal and dwell in unapproachable light. [Yet I tell you:] Approach My throne of grace with confidence, so that you may receive mercy and find grace to help in time of need.

I do not grow tired or weary; I have understanding no one can fathom. My judgments are unsearchable, My paths beyond tracing out! My thoughts are precious and vast are the sum of them! No one fully understands My mind. No one instructed Me. No one taught Me the right way. No one can compare. I hem you in before and behind. Be convinced that neither death nor life, neither angels nor demons, neither present nor the future nor any powers, neither height not depth nor anything else in all creation can separate you from My love.[10]

To this day, when I hit a tough place, I will look up verses by topic, string them together, and pray them over my life or the situation. If fearful, I string together verses on courage; if weary, verses on God's strength; if wondering what path, verses on God's anointing, favor, or wisdom.

Failure can be a footstep into your future—
if through it you learn something new
about God or yourself.

Faulty View of Ourselves

We, like those princesses in fairy tales, often ask, "Mirror, mirror on the wall, who is the fairest of them all?" A smart woman will be in a diligent pursuit of an accurate view of herself. When we see God and ourselves accurately, we are more able to make solid decisions because we are making them from an emotionally stable place. However, when we have a flawed, faulty, inconsistent, or unsound view of ourselves, we set ourselves up for an integrity lapse or we drift from our God-ordained calling.

For example, a girl with a healthy, involved father in the home earns better grades, is less likely to have premarital sex as a teen, is less likely to date an abusive man, and is less likely to drink or experiment with drugs. A healthy father helps a young woman have a healthier view of her Father in heaven.

Because I grew up with a father who didn't watch out for me, I needed to do repair work by getting to know my heavenly Father better. I spent years writing down promises of God to claim and verses about God the Father so I could capture the true essence of what a good dad and a good man looked like. Because I see myself through God's eyes and stand on His view of me, I can see my life through His eyes too.

When we find ourselves in a moment of failure, it is a good practice to ask ourselves, "Where am I off? Is it in my view of God or in my view of me?"

Below are statements that God makes about you, His child. This is what you should see in the mirror!

You Are...

Sometimes we forget to look at ourselves through God's eyes. Place this list somewhere you can see it often. You are...

The salt of the earth The light of the world	Matthew 5:13-14
More valuable than birds	Luke 12:24
In Me and I in you	John 14:20; 17:21

Already clean	John 15:3
The branches	John 15:5
My friends	John 15:14
Heirs of the prophets and of the covenant	Acts 3:25 ↳
Servants of the Most High	Acts 16:17
Called	Romans 1:6-7
Weak in your natural selves	Romans 6:19 ↳
Still worldly	1 Corinthians 3:2-4
God's fellow workers, God's field, and God's building	1 Corinthians 3:9
God's temple	1 Corinthians 3:16-17 ↳
Strong, honored	1 Corinthians 4:10
A temple of the Holy Spirit	1 Corinthians 6:19 ↳
Standing firm	1 Corinthians 10:12-13
Part of the body of Christ	1 Corinthians 12:27 ↳
A letter from Christ	2 Corinthians 3:1-3
Christ's ambassador	2 Corinthians 5:20 ↳
Sons of God	Galatians 3:26 ↳
Abraham's seed	Galatians 3:28-29 ↳
Sons, an heir	Galatians 4:6-10 6,7 ↳
Children of the promise	Galatians 4:27-28
Fellow citizens and members of God's household	Ephesians 2:19 ↳
Children of the light	Ephesians 5:8

write this in cards to Kids → (handwritten note)

Standing firm	1 Thessalonians 3:8
Sons of the light and sons of the day	1 Thessalonians 5:4-5
Slow to learn	Hebrews 5:11
Mist	James 4:14
Living stones	1 Peter 2:5
A chosen people, a royal priesthood, and a holy nation	1 Peter 2:9-10
Daughters of Sarah	1 Peter 3:6

The Train Is Pulling from the Station

So how does one recover when it feels like there's no coal in the engine, no food in the dining car, and debris on the tracks? How does a woman move forward if the train cars of her life feel like they are coming unhooked and she feels like she is unhinged, unraveling, and undone?

We start by owning our utter imperfect humanity. At the core of all of the grandeur of God, we need a humble stance. This means having a right view of ourselves—not being wrongly proud or pretentious. Humility means we bend our knees and swallow our pride and put aside our ego.

Humility is difficult. We must truly feel sorry for our sin. We live in a world where a person is rarely even sorry she got caught, much less sorry she sinned in the first place. Take courage. When you make a mistake, just admit it.

No one ever choked to death
swallowing their pride.
—Anonymous

True strength is found when we see our weaknesses and call to God, our Creator, for help! When we have a humble heart, God is motivated to respond because we have stepped off the throne and given the King His rightful place.

When we let God be our train's conductor, He can drive us out of the damage and destruction we made and into the destiny and dream He made. He is able to restore us and redeem us if we own up to our sin and ask for mercy. When we leave our rebellious and broken ways and seek His righteousness, we will find that God is full of mercy.

A woman who is completely honest, authentic, and real is a woman who is dangerous to Satan. We are not afraid of messy people or messy situations. We verbalize the hope found in kneeling at the cross. We share at a level of raw honesty, skipping all the niceties and pretenses. This cuts to the core message and rescues people out of darkness at a faster pace.

We are never stronger than when we have embraced our own weakness and asked God to extend Himself on our behalf.

Fragrance of Hope

Thanks be to God, who always leads us as captives in Christ's triumphal procession and uses us to spread the aroma of the knowledge of him everywhere. For we are to God the pleasing aroma of Christ among those who are being saved and those who are perishing. To the one we are an aroma that brings death; to the other, an aroma that brings life. And who is equal to such a task? (2 Corinthians 2:14-16).

When we are crushed, afterward our lives are a fragrance of hope, life, redemption—we are the scent of freedom! The apostle Paul got this truth!

In 1 Timothy 1:16 he says, "I was shown mercy so that in me, the worst of sinners, Christ Jesus might display his immense patience as an example for those who would believe in him and receive eternal life."

The challenge is out: Will each of us also be willing to be crushed?

Picture yourself as the oil, the fragrant perfume, poured out in humble praise to the One who freed you. That scent of life will become as dangerous as nitroglycerin because God will use your redemption story to blow sin away, break shackles, and free others held captive by their past, their shame, their guilt, their dysfunctions, and their imperfect human nature.

To become perfume, we have to submit to the crushing process.

Acknowledge God as the giver of mercy. "I will cause all my goodness to pass in front of you, and I will proclaim my name, the LORD, in your presence. I will have mercy on whom I will have mercy, and I will have compassion on whom I will have compassion" (Exodus 33:19). Step back and review God's traits and see if you have had a blurry or nonexistent view of one or more of God's attributes.

The trait of God I need to camp out in is_____

_____.

Acknowledge your sin. "Whoever conceals their sins does not prosper, but the one who confesses and renounces them finds mercy" (Proverbs 28:13). Don't make excuses or rationalize—confess.

The mistake, sin, or integrity lapse I had was _____

_____.

Ascertain your identity in Christ. How is your view of yourself not matching up to God's view of you? Looking at the mirror list, identify which definition of yourself needs to be strengthened or improved. Stand in front of a real mirror and complete this sentence out loud:

God says I am _____.

Spend time looking up verses on that topic. String them together and personalize them by placing your name right into the verses. Read it aloud twice a day until it is memorized and a part of who you are.

Amend your mistakes as much as possible. If you hurt another, apologize. If you can correct the mistake, do so. If you can make amends, try to restore the relationship. You may find new allies as you seek to make amends.

To make things right, the people I need to talk to are _____
_____ .

Actively pursue accountability. You will need people around you to build a new life. Look at your schedule and create a weekly time for this level of friendship—a space for a walk, lunch, coffee, or prayer.

I will spend more time with these people: _____
_____
_____ .

Advance in a forward plan. Pray and ask God whether you should stay put or restart somewhere else. Pray about how to keep your commitments to those you love, yet find a new way to relate to those who know your history. Bring those you love with you onto the redeemed path God will create.

There may be ramifications and consequences. Don't expect others to just forgive and forget. You will have to earn trust. Be patient with people as they learn to have confidence in you again.

I will set aside time to pray, reading God's Word and listening for His next step in my life. I will do so at this time _____
and in this place _____ .

Alter your heart. We all have the potential to blow our lives apart. We need to hate the darkness and love the light. Living in the light brings freedom to choose well. Living in the light makes us a light for God's love and a fragrance of hope!

As I walk with God, I see Him and my life more clearly.

Fragrance of Life

In the Old Testament, balm or healing oil would be used to bind up the broken, to cleanse the weary, to honor a guest, to set apart and sanctify holy temple utensils, and to anoint leaders into service. The balm or oil was also fragrant.

> Then the Lord said to Moses, "Take the following fine spices: 500 shekels of liquid myrrh, half as much…of fragrant cinnamon, 250 shekels of fragrant calamus, 500 shekels of cassia…and a hin of olive oil. Make these into a sacred anointing oil, a fragrant blend, the work of a perfumer. It will be the sacred anointing oil" (Exodus 30:22-25).

Can you smell the sweetness?

At the base of the mixture is the earthy, nutty, woody, leathery smell of dark, rich, myrrh—the same resin brought by the wise men to honor the Christ child. Mix in the homey, comforting, and seducing scent of cinnamon. This spice was linked to love and intimacy in ancient times. Then came sweet flag or aromatic cane, which most experts translate as calamus, and has an aroma close to ginger or lemon grass. Added next is cassia, which is a bark with a warm, sensual, strong cinnamon scent and is said to be a stimulant. These spices are mixed with oil and are then poured or rubbed on the skin. God prepared in detail a mixture to be associated with living a set apart, holy, sanctified life. The smell would also invoke hope as it would be used by leaders to anoint the sick to make them well.

The Anointed Life

I have a fragrance diffuser in my home. It is a beautiful vase with slivers of bamboo beautifully sprouting up from the sweet-scented oil. But to keep the aroma, I must keep the decanter filled. In the same way, if we allow the Spirit of God to reign, healing will come. To gain the full potential of the anointed life, we must remain humble.

One woman in the Bible gave an extraordinary picture of humility and contrition before Jesus:

> A woman in that town who lived a sinful life learned that Jesus was eating at the Pharisee's house, so she came there with an alabaster jar of perfume. As she stood behind him at his feet weeping, she began to wet his feet with her tears. Then she wiped them with her hair, kissed them and poured perfume on them (Luke 7:37-38).

It was likely this perfume was very expensive, made of the best ingredients, and valued at a year's wages. She sacrificed greatly to honor Christ. Some scholars point to her overwhelming gratitude—her tears falling into the perfume and her falling to Christ's feet—as a perfectly timed gift to bolster Christ before He headed to the cross. The fragrant oil was also used to prepare a body for burial. Her anointing of the Anointed One brings to us the possibility of living an anointed life!

Your Life: A Fragrant Aroma

The aroma process often begins with beautiful, fragrant plants, but the perfuming process is typically explained with words like *crushing*, *mashing*, *pressing*, *squeezing*, *sifting*, and *heating*! And many aromas only come through after being heated or burned. In ancient times, aroma can also mean incense (wood soaked in fragrant oils or resin then burned). The word *perfume* has at its root the Latin word *fumus*, which means *smoke*. It is interesting that our life's work will be tested by fire:

> If anyone builds on this foundation using gold, silver, costly stones, wood, hay or straw, their work will be shown for what it is, because the Day will bring it to light. It will be revealed with fire, and the fire will test the quality of each person's work. If what has been built survives, the builder will receive a reward (1 Corinthians 3:12-14).

After we have come "through the smoke," what remains is exquisite. So whether by crushing or fire, the point is made that our lives become more fragrant as we submit to the process of refinement at the hands of our Maker.

As an act of worship for all God has taught you through *7 Simple Skills for Every Woman*, select a fragrance or scent to symbolize God's design for your life. What bouquet would capture Christ's redemptive work in your life?

To mark a season when God liberated me from a difficult circumstance, I wore a perfume called Amazing Grace all year. The scent consistently reminded me to the praise the One who can make the broken beautiful. Go to a perfume counter or fragrance shop or talk with an essential oils distributor to locate a scent that captures the beauty of how you feel when you live set free.

May your life be a fragrant offering of love toward God, and the fragrance of hope and love to all whose lives intersect with yours. A life hidden in God's love is simply beautiful!

> Yes, Lord, walking in the way of your laws, we wait for you;
> your name and renown are the desire of our hearts (Isaiah 26:8).

Notes

Chapter 1

1. This story is also related in my book *LOL with God: Devotional Messages of Hope & Humor for Women* (Wheaton, IL: Tyndale, 2010).

2. "Universal Decay and Conservation of Matter/Energy," *Creation Science Today,* accessed September 11, 2014, http://creationsciencetoday.com/02-Universal_Decay.html.

3. "Work Stress on the Rise," *Huffington Post,* April 10, 2013, http://www.huffingtonpost.com/2013/04/10/work-stress-jobs-americans_n_3053428.html.

4. Kate Harris, "Wonder Women—Are We Really Satisfied with Life?" *Women Doing Well* (blog), June 25, 2014, http://www.inspiringgenerousjoy.org/2014/06/25/wonder-women-are-we-really-satisfied-with-life/.

5. Sharon Jayson, "Who's Feeling Stressed? Young Adults, New Survey Shows," *USA Today,* February 7, 2013, http://www.usatoday.com/story/news/nation/2013/02/06/stress-psychology-millennials-depression/1878295/.

6. Anthony Robbins, foreword to *The Compound Effect*, by Darren Hardy (New York: Vanguard Press, 2012).

Chapter 2

1. Deborah Cruz, "Top 10 Most Outlandish Helicopter Parent Moves," *The Stir,* February 27, 2012, http://thestir.cafemom.com/toddler/133655.

2. Rachael Rettner, "Helicopter Parents Have Neurotic Kids," *NBC News,* June 3, 2010, http://www.nbcnews.com/id/37493795.

3. Bonnie Rochman, "Hover No More," *Time,* February 22, 2013, http://healthland.time.com/2013/02/22/hover.

4. Dave Mosher, "Daily Decisions Make Mush of Your Mind," *LiveScience,* April 18, 2008, http://www.livescience.com/2453-daily-decisions-mush-mind.html.

5. Michael F. Roizen and Mehmet C. Oz, *You on a Diet* (New York: Free Press, 2006).

6. Mosher, "Daily Decisions."

7. Gari Meacham, *Watershed Moments* (Grand Rapids, MI: Zondervan, 2013).

8. *Hearings on Constitutional Amendments Relating to Abortion, Before the Senate Judiciary Subcommittee,* 97th Cong. (October 19, 1981) (statement of Jasper Williams, Jr., M.D., Past President of the National Medical Association).

9. Don Sloan and Paula Hartz, *Choice* (New York: International Publishers, 2002), 46.

10. Patrick Johnson, "Are There Rare Cases When an Abortion Is Justified?" *Association of Prolife Physicians*, March 31, 2009, http://prolifephysicians.org/app/?p=59.

11. Rebecca Downs, "A Pro-Life View During Sexual Assault Awareness Month," *Life News*, April 24, 2012, http://www.lifenews.com/2012/04/24/a-pro-life-view.

12. Amy Sobie, "What About Abortion in Cases of Rape and Incest? Women and Sexual Assault," *Life News*, April 5, 2010, http://www.lifenews.com/2010/04/05/nat-6223/.

13. Gwen Smith, *Broken into Beautiful* (Eugene, OR: Harvest House Publishers, 2008), 160.

14. Robert Fleischmann, "Sobering Statistics on Abortion," *Christian Life Resources* 31, no. 1 (2011), http://www.christianliferesources.com?9244.

15. Michael Krogerus and Roman Tchappeler, *The Decisions Book* (New York: W.W. Norton & Company, 2008), 118.

16. Bob Pritchett, *Fire Someone Today* (Nashville, TN: Thomas Nelson, 2006), 24.

Chapter 3

1. Bill Farrel, *The 10 Best Decisions a Man Can Make* (Eugene, OR: Harvest House Publishers, 2010).

2. Michael Krogerus and Roman Tchappeler, *The Decisions Book* (New York: W.W. Norton & Company, 2008), 22-23.

Chapter 4

1. "Research." *Back to the Bible*, www.backtothebible.org/research.

Chapter 5

1. Leslie Vernick, *The Emotionally Destructive Relationship* (Eugene, OR: Harvest House Publishers, 2007), 27-28.

Chapter 6

1. Mike Ashcraft and Rachel Olsen, *My One Word* (Grand Rapids, MI: Zondervan, 2012), 37-38.

Chapter 7

1. Ellie Kay, personal e-mail interview, October 2014.

2. David Hinckley, "Average American Watches 5 Hours of TV Per Day, Report Shows," *New York Daily News*, March 5, 2014, http://nydn.us/1fHRJee.

3. Archibald D. Hart and Sylvia H. Frejd, *The Digital Invasion* (Grand Rapids, MI: Baker Books, 2013).

4. Deanna Michalopoulos, "How the Average Woman Spends Her Day," *Women's Health Magazine*, August 7, 2006, http://www.womenshealthmag.com/you-and-improved/statistics-for-the-average-woman.

5. Marcia Ramsland, personal e-mail interview, October 2014.

6. Bill Farrel, *The 10 Best Decisions a Man Can Make* (Eugene, OR: Harvest House Publishers, 2010), 37.

7. Bruce Feiler, "The Stories That Bind Us," *The New York Times,* March 15, 2013 http://www.nytimes.com/2013/03/17/fashion/the-family-stories-that-bind-us-this-life.html.

8. Pam Farrel, *Woman of Influence* (Downer's Grove, IL: InterVarsity Press, 1996), 99.

9. "Eden, CO Train Disaster," *Alamosa Journal*, August 12, 1904, http://www3.gendisasters.com/colorado/5752/eden-train-disaster-over-100-lives-lost.

10. Farrel, *Woman of Influence,* 67-68.

Pam Farrel and her husband, Bill, are the authors of *Men Are Like Waffles—Women Are Like Spaghetti* (over 300,000 copies sold) and *Red-Hot Monogamy*. In addition, Pam has written *52 Ways to Wow Your Husband* and *The 10 Best Decisions a Woman Can Make*. They are cofounders and codirectors of Love-Wise, an organization to help people connect love and wisdom and bring practical insights to their personal relationships.

52 Ways to Wow Your Husband

How to Put a Smile on His Face

PAM FARREL

Men Are Like Waffles—Women Are Like Spaghetti

52 Ways to Wow Your Husband

With the same candor and creativity that made *Men Are Like Waffles—Women Are Like Spaghetti* a bestseller, author Pam Farrel gives wives 52 ways to wow their husbands and add spark to their marriages. Pam delivers humor in her fun woman-to-woman style through inspirational stories, godly advice, and easy-to-read offerings that include:

- wow assignments: simple ways to support, love, and encourage husbands
- wow wisdom: Bible verses and wisdom to help women cover their spouse with prayer
- wow dates: creative ideas for everything from shared meals to weekend getaways

Newlyweds, married with kids, or empty nesters will appreciate these ideas crafted for the busy life. A woman can try one idea a week for a year or take on a few at a time to deepen her spiritual, emotional, and physical bond with her loved one.

Men Are Like Waffles
Women Are Like
Spaghetti

Understanding and Delighting in Your Differences

Bill and Pam Farrel

Men Are Like Waffles—Women Are Like Spaghetti

With over 300,000 copies sold, bestselling authors Bill and Pam Farrel help you find the humor in yourself as you gain biblical wisdom, solid insight, and workable skills to help your relationships flourish—all served up in just the right combination so that readers can feast on enticing ways to

- keep communication cooking
- let gender differences work for—not against—them
- help each other relieve stress
- achieve fulfillment in romantic relationships
- coordinate parenting so kids get the best of both Mom and Dad

The Farrels explain why a man is like a waffle (each element of his life is in a separate box) and a woman is like spaghetti (everything in her life touches everything else). End-of-chapter questions and exercises make this unique and fun look at the different ways men and women regard life a terrific tool for not only marriage, but also for a reader's relationships at work, at home, at church, and with friends.

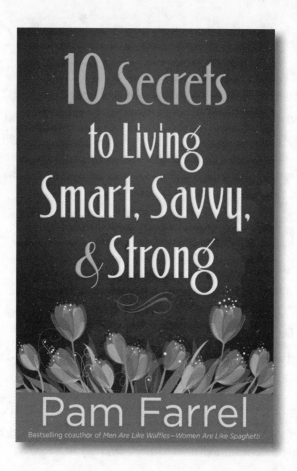

10 Secrets
to Living
Smart, Savvy,
& Strong

Pam Farrel

10 Secrets to Living Smart, Savy, and Strong

Pam Farrel points the way for women in midlife to live smart, savvy, and strong during this exciting and demanding season. Insights on relationships, health, menopause, finances, and more are infused with biblical wisdom and loads of humor. Readers will discover how to

- trust God in more fulfilling ways with life-impacting decisions
- be at peace with new physical, mental, and emotional changes
- benefit from diet, exercise, and relationships to maximize midlife and beyond

Designed for personal use or group study, *10 Secrets to Living Smart, Savvy, and Strong* will empower those baby-boomer women who seek life-enhancing wisdom to get the most out of this time of their lives.

To learn more about Harvest House books and
to read sample chapters, visit our website:

www.harvesthousepublishers.com

HARVEST HOUSE PUBLISHERS
EUGENE, OREGON